KNOCK KNOCK!

Jokes for all the Family

Fred Fox

summersdale

KNOCK KNOCK

Text contributed by Sarah Herman and Marcia Allison

Summersdale Publishers Ltd
46 West Street
Chichester
West Sussex
PO19 1RP
UK

www.summersdale.com

Printed and bound in Great Britain

ISBN: 978-1-84024-781-7

Substantial discounts on bulk quantities of Summersdale books are available to corporations, professional associations and other organisations. For details telephone Summersdale Publishers on (+44-1243-771107), fax (+44-1243-786300) or email (nicky@summersdale.com).

Contents

Knock Knock

Knock knock!

Who's there?

Old lady.

Old lady who?

I didn't know you could yodel!

Knock knock!

Who's there?

Doris.

Doris who?

Doris locked, that's why I'm knocking!

Knock knock!

Who's there?

Police.

Police who?

Police let me in, it's freezing out here!

Knock knock!

Who's there?

Luke.

Luke who?

Luke through the window and you'll see!

Knock knock!

Who's there?

Norma Lee.

Norma Lee who?

Norma Lee you remember who I am.

Knock knock!

Who's there?

I Dunnop.

I Dunnop who?

Knock knock!

Who's there?

Woody.

Woody who?

Woody like to come out and play?

Knock knock!

Who's there?

Tank.

Tank who?

You're welcome!

Knock knock!

Who's there?

Wendy.

Wendy who?

**Wendy red red robin comes bob bob bobbin'
along...**

Knock knock!

Who's there?

Aardvark.

Aardvark who?

Aardvark to my house, but it's too far away.

Knock knock!

Who's there?

Madam.

Madam who?

Madam foot is caught in the door!

Knock knock!

Who's there?

Hawaii.

Hawaii who?

I'm fine, Hawaii you?

Knock knock!

Who's there?

Who.

Who who?

Is there an owl in there?

Knock knock!

Who's there?

Anita!

Anita who?

Anita show you something!

Knock knock!

Who's there?

Pecan.

Pecan who?

Pecan someone your own size!

Knock knock!

Who's there?

Dexter.

Dexter who?

Dexter halls with boughs of holly.

Knock knock!

Who's there?

Annie.

Annie who?

Annie thing you can do, I can do better.

Knock knock!

Who's there?

Boo.

Boo who?

Don't cry. It's only a joke.

Knock knock!

Who's there?

Lettuce.

Lettuce who?

Lettuce in and all will be revealed!

Knock knock!

Who's there?

Caesar.

Caesar who?

Caesar jolly good fellow!

Knock knock!

Who's there?

Celeste.

Celeste who?

Celeste time I lend you money!

Knock knock!

Who's there?

Myth.

Myth who?

Myth you, too!

Knock knock!

Who's there?

Dewey.

Dewey who?

Dewey have to go to the doctor's?

Knock knock!

Who's there?

Cherry.

Cherry who?

Cherry oh, see you later!

Knock knock!

Who's there?

Chester.

Chester who?

Chester minute, don't you recognise me?

Knock knock!

Who's there?

Chicken.

Chicken who?

Chicken the oven, I can smell burning!

Knock knock!

Who's there?

Cereal.

Cereal who?

Cereal pleasure to meet you!

Knock knock!

Who's there?

Congo.

Congo who?

Congo out, I'm grounded!

Knock knock!

Who's there?

Don.

Don who?

Don mess about, just open the door!

Knock knock!

Who's there?

Eamon.

Eamon who?

Eamon my birthday suit, let me in!

Knock knock!

Who's there?

Esther.

Esther who?

Esther anything I can do for you?

Knock knock!

Who's there?

Fanny.

Fanny who?

Fanny body calls, I'm out!

Knock knock!

Who's there?

Gladys.

Gladys who?

Gladys the weekend, aren't you?

Knock knock!

Who's there?

Gopher.

Gopher who?

Gopher a long walk off a short pier!

Knock knock!

Who's there?

Hatch.

Hatch who?

Bless you!

Knock knock!

Who's there?

Mickey.

Mickey who?

Mickey's stuck in the lock!

Knock knock!

Who's there?

Theodore.

Theodore who?

Theodore is stuck and it won't open!

Knock knock!

Who's there?

Nana.

Nana who?

Nana your business!

Knock knock!

Who's there?

Radio.

Radio who?

Radio not, here I come!

Knock knock!

Who's there?

Venice.

Venice who?

Venice it dinner time?

Knock knock!

Who's there?

Onya.

Onya who?

Onya marks, get set, go!

Knock, knock!

Who's there?

Ivan.

Ivan who?

Ivan infectious disease.

Knock, knock!

Who's there?

Ewan.

Ewan who?

Ewan me need to have a little chat.

Knock knock!

Who's there?

Egbert.

Egbert who?

Egbert no bacon please!

Knock knock!

Who's there?

Ivor.

Ivor who?

Ivor special delivery!

Knock, knock!

Who's there?

Shirley.

Shirley who?

Shirley you're tired of all these 'knock knock' jokes by now?!

Funny Family

A family is like a box of chocolates.

They're mostly sweet, with a few nuts.

A man went to the doctor for a check up and was told he had high blood pressure. 'It runs in the family,' he said. 'On your mother or father's side?' asked the doctor. 'Neither,' the man replied, 'it's on my wife's side.' The doctor, confused, asked, 'How can your wife's family give you high blood pressure?' The man replied, 'You try spending the weekend with them and you'll see.'

A boy asked his father, 'Dad, what's an idiot?' His father replied, 'An idiot is a man or woman who explains their ideas and thoughts in such a long and convoluted way that the other person they're trying to explain things to can't understand them at all. Do you understand me?' 'No,' said his son.

How do you make antifreeze?

Steal her pyjamas.

What's the difference between bogeys and broccoli?

Children won't eat broccoli.

After years of wondering, a man who
never understood why he looked so
different from his brother and sister asked
his mother if he'd been adopted. 'Yes, you
were,' said his mother, 'but unfortunately
it didn't work out so they
sent you back.'

A man was in the supermarket with his baby son who wouldn't stop screaming. As he went around the supermarket he could be heard saying, 'Calm down John, calm down. Don't scream John, everything's going to be OK.' When he reached the checkout a lady in line gestured towards the pushchair and said, 'You're doing a great job soothing little John.' The man replied, 'My baby's called Max. My name's John.'

A woman carrying a baby passed the conductor as she got on the train. 'Oh my God!' cried the conductor, 'That is the ugliest-looking baby I think I've ever seen.' Shocked, the woman made her way to her seat and sat down. She said to the man next to her, 'The conductor was just extremely rude to me.' The man replied, 'You should go and tell the driver. I'll hold your pet monkey for you.'

A teenage girl had been chatting on the phone for about an hour before she hung up. Her father, impressed, said, 'That was a quick chat for you – you're usually on that thing for at least two hours.' His daughter smiled and said, 'Oh, it was a wrong number.'

Two four-year-old boys were overheard talking in the playground. 'My dad is a teacher. What does your daddy do?' asked the first boy. 'My daddy's a lawyer,' answered the second boy. 'Honest?' asked the first. 'No, just the normal kind,' replied the second boy.

A man is at the local swimming pool with his children, when he overhears the lifeguard shouting at his son. Turning to the boy's dad the furious lifeguard says, 'Your son was peeing in the swimming pool, and it's just not acceptable.' 'Oh, come on,' says the dad, 'all kids pee in the pool occasionally.' The lifeguard replies, 'Not from the diving board.'

Three naughty boys were hanging out at the zoo when the zookeeper walked over and asked them their names and what they were up to. 'My name's Joe and I'm feeding peanuts to the lions,' said the first boy. 'My name's George and I'm also feeding peanuts to the lions,' said the second. 'And what's your name?' the zookeeper said to the third boy. 'Peanuts,' he replied.

After staring at her granddad's wrinkly old face, a little girl asked, 'Granddad, did God make you?' 'Yes, he did – a long time ago,' replied her granddad. 'And did he make me?' 'Yes, although that was more recently,' he explained. The girl thought and then said, 'God's doing a much better job these days, isn't he?'

Teenager: Mum, can I please wear a bra?

Mum: No.

Teenager: Why? I'm nearly fifteen years old!

Mum: I won't say it again David, no!

Father: I think our son gets all his brains from me.

Mother: You're probably right. I still have all mine.

Jane: Do you have a grandfather?

Simon: No, but he's OK.

Hopping Mad

What kind of shoes do frogs like?

Open toad sandals.

Why did the frog say 'bark'?

He was learning a foreign language.

What did the frog order at the burger bar?

French flies and a diet croak.

What's green and tough?

A frog with a machine gun.

What happened to the illegally parked frog?

He got toad away.

What was the amphibian's job on the cruise liner?

He was the froghorn.

What did the bus driver say to the frog?

Hop on.

What's green and spins round really fast?

A frog in a blender.

What's yellow and spins round really fast?

A mouldy frog in a blender.

How do frogs die?
They Kermit suicide.

What's a frog's favourite flower?
A croakus.

Where do toads keep their money?
In a river bank.

What's a frog's favourite lawn game?
Croak-et.

What do frogs drink?
Hot croako with marshmallows.

What's green and slimy and found at the North Pole?
A lost frog.

How did the toad die?
He simply croaked.

What goes dot-dot-croak, dot-dash-croak?
Morse toad.

Where do frogs leave their hats and coats?

In the croakroom.

What kind of pole is short and floppy?

A tadpole.

Why didn't the tadpole have any friends?

Because he was newt to the area.

School Days

Why did the teacher wear sunglasses to work?

Because his class was so bright.

After noticing a child in her class pulling faces, a primary school teacher took the troublemaker aside and said, 'When I was little my mummy told me if I pulled faces the wind would change and it would get stuck that way.' The naughty boy replied, 'Well, miss, you can't say you weren't warned.'

Why did the boy hit his test paper with a tennis racket?

He wanted to ace the exam.

What do opticians and teachers have in common?

They both test pupils.

Why isn't whispering permitted in class?

Because it's not aloud.

Did you hear about the devil-worshipper who was really bad at spelling?

He sold his soul to Santa.

Katie was late for school every day, so one morning her teacher asked her why. 'Because of the sign,' Katie said. 'What sign?' replied her teacher. 'The sign that says, "School ahead, go slow".'

Pupil: Miss, I think number six is scared of seven.

Teacher: Why is that?

Pupil: Because seven eight nine.

Teacher: Do you have trouble making decisions?

Pupil: Well… yes and no.

Teacher: Which two days of the week start with the letter 't'?

Pupil: Today and tomorrow.

Teacher: You will be allowed thirty minutes for each question.

Pupil: How long do we get to write the answers?

Teacher: Who gave you that black eye, Robert?

Robert: No one gave it to me, sir, I fought really hard for it.

A girl raises her hand in class and asks the teacher if she can answer the call of nature. The teacher excuses her and the girl leaves the room. Seconds later, she is back. Impressed at how fast her classmate has managed to take care of business, her friend asks her how she did it so quickly. The girl replies, 'It was a prank call.'

Pupil: Sir, my dog ate my homework.

Teacher: And where's your dog now?

Pupil: He's at the vet's – he doesn't like maths either.

A boy came home from school and told his mother he couldn't do science any more. 'Why not?' asked his mother. 'Because I blew something up,' explained her son. 'What?' she said. 'The school,' he replied.

Why did the student say his marks were 'underwater'?

Because they were below C level.

Why did the student write on his toes in class?

He was trying to think on his feet.

Why did the school boy wear stilts?

Because he went to a high school.

Why couldn't the student divide by two?

She didn't know the half of it.

A teacher was taking his first class at a new school. After introducing himself he announced: 'Stand up if you think you're stupid.' Nobody moved, and then after a minute, one pupil stood up. 'So you think you're an idiot, then?' said the teacher. 'No,' replied the pupil, 'I just didn't want you standing up all on your own.'

Did you hear about the schoolboy who put clean socks on every day?

By Friday he couldn't get his shoes on.

Did you hear about the teacher who was cross-eyed?

He couldn't control his pupils.

Why did the schoolgirl only wear one glove?

Because on the weather forecast it said it might be warm, but on the other hand it could be cooler.

What kind of exams do cows take?

Hay Levels.

**Mother: Why was your exam score so low
last week?**

Son: Absence.

Mother: What, you missed the exam?

Son: No, but the girl who sits next to me did.

At a parent's evening a teacher told her pupil's
father, 'Well, there's one good thing I can say about
your son.' The father asked, 'What's that?' The
teacher responded, 'With grades this bad, there's no
way he's cheating.'

Pupil: What's the date today?

Examiner: That's not important, get on with the test.

Pupil: But sir, I want to get something right.

Child: My music teacher said my singing was out of this world.

Mum: Really?

Child: Well, she said it was 'unearthly'.

Teacher: 'Francis, conjugate the verb "to walk" in the simple present tense.'

Francis: 'I walk… um… You walk…'

Teacher: 'Quicker please, Francis.'

Francis: 'I jog… You jog…'

In an exam room the teacher snapped at one pupil, 'Andy, I hope I didn't just see you looking at Jane's test paper?' Andy replied, 'I hope you didn't see me either.'

Teacher: Can anyone use the word 'fascinate' in a sentence?

Pupil: My dad bought a new shirt with nine buttons, but he's so fat he was only able to fasten eight.

Lucy: Miss, can I go to the toilet?

Teacher: Lucy, *may* I go to the toilet?

Lucy: I asked first!

A teacher arrived late to class and saw an unflattering caricature of himself on the blackboard. Turning to the class he asked, 'Who was responsible for this grossness?' Sniggering, the class joker replied, 'Well, I really can't be sure, but I blame the parents.'

A son told his father he couldn't go to school because he didn't feel very well. 'Where don't you feel very well?' his father asked. 'In school,' the boy replied.

Why did the primary school teacher marry the caretaker?

He swept her off her feet.

What did the school tie say to the cap?

You go on a head while I hang around.

Teacher: How many seconds are there in a year?

Pupil: Twelve! January the 2nd, February the 2nd...

Pupil: I don't think I deserved zero for this exam.

Teacher: Me neither. But I couldn't give you any lower.

Teacher: Whenever I ask you a question, I want you to answer altogether. What is nine times four?

Class: Altogether!

Teacher: What is the longest word in the English language?

Pupil: Smiles – because there's a whole mile between the first and last letter.

Teacher: Where in England is Felixstowe?

Pupil: On the end of Felix's foot.

Teacher: What did Henry VIII do when he came to the throne?

Pupil: He sat on it.

Doctor, Doctor

Doctor, doctor, I can't stop my hands from shaking.

Do you drink a lot?

Not really – I spill most of it!

Doctor, doctor, I feel like a racehorse.

Take one of these every four laps.

Doctor, doctor, I keep getting pains in my eye when I drink coffee.

Have you tried taking the spoon out?

Doctor, doctor, have you got something for a bad headache?

Of course. Just take this hammer and hit yourself on the head.

Doctor, doctor, I think I'm a dog.

Why don't you sit on the sofa so we can talk about it?

But I'm not allowed on the sofa!

Doctor, doctor, I keep thinking I'm a goat.

How long have you felt like this?

Ever since I was a kid.

Doctor, doctor, there's a carrot growing in my ear.

How did that happen?

I don't know – I planted cauliflowers.

Doctor, doctor, I keep seeing double.

Please sit on the couch.

Which one?

Doctor, doctor, I've lost my memory!

When did this happen?

When did what happen?

Doctor, doctor, my wife thinks she's a goose.

Send her in to see me.

I can't, she's flown south for the winter.

Doctor, doctor, will this ointment clear up my spots?

I never make rash promises!

Doctor, doctor, since my operation I've had two heartbeats.

Ah, so that's where my wristwatch went!

Doctor, doctor, you've taken out my tonsils, my gall bladder and my appendix, but I still feel ill.

That's quite enough out of you!

Doctor, doctor, I can't stop trembling.

I'll be with you in a couple of shakes.

Doctor, doctor, I keep hearing ringing in my ears.

Nonsense, you're as sound as a bell.

Doctor, doctor, what do you charge for treating a split personality?

Fifteen pounds each.

Doctor, doctor, what do you recommend for flat feet?

Try a foot pump.

Doctor, doctor, I need something for my kidneys.

This isn't a butcher's.

Doctor, doctor, my aunt has a sore throat.

Give her this bottle of auntie-septic.

Doctor, doctor, my eyesight is getting worse.

It certainly is – this is the post office.

Doctor, doctor, my mind keeps wandering.

Don't worry – it's too weak to go very far.

Doctor, doctor, I'm just not myself.

Yes – I noticed the improvement.

Doctor, doctor, what are my chances of losing weight?

Slim, madam.

Doctor, doctor, when I get up in the morning, I'm always dizzy for half an hour.

Try getting up half an hour later.

Doctor, doctor, my sister thinks she is a lift!

Well, tell her to come in.

I can't – she doesn't stop at this floor!

Doctor, doctor, I keep seeing purple and yellow spots.

Have you seen an optician?

No – just purple and yellow spots.

Doctor, doctor, my husband thinks he's a car.

Show him in at once.

I can't – he's double parked.

Doctor, doctor, my daughter thinks she's an actress.

Don't worry – it's just a stage she's going through.

Doctor, doctor, I can't stop robbing banks.

Sit down and I'll take a few notes.

Doctor, doctor, I can't stop shoplifting.

Have you taken anything for it?

Doctor, doctor, I'm only four feet tall.

You'll just have to be a little patient.

Doctor, doctor, I'm suffering from amnesia.

Take these pills and you'll soon forget all about it.

Doctor, doctor, I'm terrified of milk chocolate.

Another fruit and nut case!

Doctor, doctor, I can't get to sleep.

Sit on the edge of the bed and you'll soon drop off.

Doctor, doctor, I'm going to die in 51 seconds!

I will be with you in a minute!

Doctor, doctor, can I have a second opinion?

Of course, come back tomorrow.

Doctor, doctor, I can't stop telling lies.

You don't expect me to believe that, do you?

Doctor, doctor, I've got wind! Can you give me something?

Yes – here's a kite!

Doctor, doctor, I've a terrible problem. Can you help me out?

Certainly – which way did you come in?

Doctor, doctor, I've been stung by a bee. Shall I put some ointment on it?

Don't be silly – it must be miles away by now.

Doctor, doctor, I think I'm having déjà vu!
Didn't I see you yesterday?

Doctor, doctor, my little boy has just swallowed a roll of film.
Don't panic – call me back if anything develops.

Doctor, doctor, I think I'm a telephone.
Well, take these pills and if they don't work then give me a ring.

Doctor, doctor, I think I've been bitten by a vampire.

Drink this glass of water.

Will it make me better?

No, but I'll be able to see if your neck leaks.

Doctor, doctor, I'm having trouble pronouncing 'F's, 'T's and 'H's.

Well, you can't say fairer than that then.

Doctor, doctor, I feel like a pair of curtains.

Pull yourself together!

Check the Scales

Why wouldn't the lizard go on the weighing machine?

Because he had his own scales.

What subject do snakes love at school?
Hisssssstory.

Why are snakes hard to fool?
They have no legs to pull.

What do snake couples have on their bath towels?
Hiss and Hers.

What did the python say to the viper?
I've got a crush on you.

What's the best thing about deadly snakes?

They've got poisonality.

Why did the python do national service?

He was coiled up.

Why did the viper viper nose?

Because the adder adder handkerchief.

What do you give a sick snake?

Asp-rin.

What do baby pythons play with?

Rattle snakes.

What's long, green and goes hith?

A snake with a lisp.

Which snakes are found on cars?

Windscreen vipers.

When Noah said, 'Go forth and multiply!' why didn't the snakes?

They were adders.

What kind of tiles can't you stick on walls?

Reptiles.

Best of Blonde

How does a blonde make up her mind?

She puts lipstick on her forehead.

If a blonde and a brunette did a parachute jump, who would make it to the ground first?

The brunette, because the blonde would have to stop for directions.

What should you do if a blonde hurls a pin at you?

Run as far away from her as you can – she's still holding the grenade.

Why did the blonde jump in the pool fully clothed?

There was a mirror at the bottom of the pool.

If a one-armed blonde is hanging from a tree, how do you make her fall?

Wave.

Three blondes were on a hiking adventure. While walking through a field they came across some tracks. The first blonde said, 'I think these are bear tracks.' The second blonde had a look and said, 'I think they're moose tracks.' So the third blonde crouched down over the tracks to investigate, and got run over by a train.

Why did the blonde crash the helicopter?

She was cold, so she turned off the 'ceiling fan'.

Why don't blondes get lunch breaks at work?

It takes too long to retrain them afterwards.

Why did the blonde take a tape measure to bed?

To see how long she slept.

Why did the blonde girl take sixteen friends with her to the cinema?

Because it said 'Under fifteen not admitted' on the sign.

A blonde walked into a clothes store and asked if she could borrow a hanger to unlock her car because she'd locked her keys inside. The shop assistant obliged, and a few minutes later went out into the car park to see if the blonde needed any help. Outside the car the blonde girl was furiously trying to open the door, and inside was her blonde friend shouting, 'A bit to the left, wait, a bit to the right!'

What's the best way to make sure your blonde girlfriend's laughing on Thursday?

Tell her a joke on Monday.

Why did the blonde stand in front of the mirror with her eyes closed?

Because she wanted to see what she looked like when she slept.

What do you call a blonde with half a brain?

Gifted.

Why did the blonde only listen to her radio in the morning?

Because it was an AM radio.

Tired of being referred to as a dumb blonde, Amy dyed her hair black and drove out into the country for the afternoon. She pulled up at a farm where there were lots of cute lambs in the field. She greeted the farmer and said, 'If I can guess exactly how many lambs you have, can I take one home?' The farmer agreed. '139,' said the blonde. It was the right answer so the shocked farmer kept his promise and the blonde picked out a lamb and walked back to her car. Then the farmer appeared at her car window and said, 'If I can guess your natural hair colour, can I have my dog back?'

A blonde was on a tour of a national park, when the tour guide explained how many dinosaur fossils had been found in the area they were standing. 'Really?!' the blonde exclaimed. 'I can't believe the dinosaurs would come so close to the main road!'

A blonde calls the fire station because her flat has gone up in flames. The dispatcher asks her how to get to her house. 'Are you people idiots?' she replies. 'In your big red lorry, of course!'

Why did the blonde sell her car?

For petrol money.

What's the difference between the Loch Ness Monster and a smart blonde?

Maybe, someday, we'll find the Monster.

Why did the blonde ask to move away from the window seat on the plane?

Because she'd just had her hair done and she didn't want it to get messed up.

Why are blondes and pumpkins so similar?

They both have hollowed-out heads.

In the science round of a general knowledge quiz, a blonde is asked, 'If you were in a vacuum and someone called your name, would you be able to hear them?' The blonde thinks for a while, and then says, 'Is it on or off?'

A blonde was driving home when she spotted another blonde trying to row a boat in a field. She jumped out the car and shouted, 'It's blondes like you who give the rest of us a bad name! If I could swim I'd come out there and hit you on your dumb blonde head!'

Why do blondes have more fun?

Because it takes less to entertain them.

It took a blonde four months to finish a jigsaw, but she was still really excited. Well, it did say 2–4 years on the box.

How do you convince a blonde to go up on the roof?

Tell her the drinks are on the house.

Why did the blonde creep past the medicine cabinet?

She wanted to make sure she didn't wake up the sleeping tablets.

A blonde and a brunette were watching the evening news. One of the stories was about a man threatening to jump off a cliff. The blonde bet the brunette fifty pounds that the man wouldn't jump, but sure enough he jumped to his death. When the blonde tried to hand over the money to her friend the brunette admitted she'd already seen the story on the lunch-time news programme. 'So did I,' said the blonde, 'But I didn't think he would jump again!'

Why was the blonde's ear burnt?

She answered her mobile while she was ironing.

Why should you never give M&Ms to a blonde?

She'll try and put them in alphabetical order.

What's yellow and five miles long, with an IQ of thirty-five?

A blonde parade.

A pizza waitress asked the blonde if she would like her pizza cut up into six pieces or twelve pieces. 'Six, please,' she said, 'I could never eat twelve.'

What's the best way to keep a blonde occupied all day?

Write 'Please turn over' on both sides of a piece of paper.

What's the term for a blonde who dyes her hair brown?

Artificial Intelligence.

What's another term for a smart blonde?

A golden retriever.

Two blondes were sitting in the park. One says, 'Oh my goodness, look at that man with one eye!' The other blonde covers one of her eyes and says, 'Where?'

A man came home to find his blonde wife decorating the living room wearing a denim jacket with her expensive fur coat over the top. 'Why aren't you wearing overalls, or an old shirt?' asked the confused husband. 'Look,' said his wife, showing him the paint tin, 'It says for best results, put on two coats.'

Why was the blonde staring at the carton of orange juice?

It said 'concentrate' on the label.

Why was the blonde dancing on the sink?

She wanted to try out tap.

A blonde stopped a man in the street to ask him the time. He told her it was 5.45 p.m. Clearly confused, the blonde said, 'It's so weird, I've been asking people that question all day, and everyone has given me a different answer.'

Football Funnies

Why do magicians make great footballers?

Because they do hat-tricks.

Why don't they build football stadiums on the moon?

Because there's no atmosphere.

What happened when the footballer took a corner?

He turned the pitch into a triangle.

Why should you never invite a football player to your dinner party?

Because he would spend the whole time dribbling.

What's a footballer's favourite tea?

Penaltea.

James was late for school. When his teacher asked him why James replied, 'Sorry, Miss, I was dreaming about a football match.' She looked confused and said, 'But that still doesn't explain why you're late.' He replied, 'There was extra time.'

Manager: The team's new winger cost ten million. I call him our wonder player.

Fan: Why's that? Is he really good?

Manager: No. It's because when I watch him play, I wonder why I bought him.

Why are footballers such good dancers?

Because they have so many foot balls.

What's black and white and black and white and black and white?

A Newcastle fan rolling down a hill.

What's red, white and smiling?

The Sunderland fan who pushed him.

Why did the footballer take a jump rope onto the pitch with him?

Because he was the skipper.

What's a Birmingham City fan's least favourite ice cream flavour?

Aston Vanilla.

Why did the chicken cross the football pitch?

To egg on the players.

Why did the duck get sent off the pitch?

For fowl play.

Why did the dog hate playing football?

Because he was a boxer.

Why should you never play football against a group of big cats?

They might be cheetahs.

How do you know when it's a cup draw?

The managers sit round sketching crockery.

What does the goalie like to do when he's had a bad game?

Hit the bars.

Why don't most bankers like regular football?

They prefer fiver-side.

After resigning from a football club the manager gave a press conference. 'And how did the crowd react?' asked one journalist. 'Were they behind you?' The ex-manager replied, 'They were right behind me, the whole lot of them, but I managed to lose them at the motorway roundabout.'

Manager: What do you have to say for yourselves? You finished bottom out of twenty teams.

Player: Well, it could've been worse.

Manager: How, exactly?!

Player: There could've been more teams.

Schoolboy: The ref sent me off.

Mum: What for?

Schoolboy: The rest of the game.

Why didn't the sandwich show up to football training?

Because he was only a sub.

Why will an artist never win a game of football?

Because they keep drawing.

What did the footballer's wife say when she went to the World Cup Final?

The world would never fit in that cup.

Bear Naked Teddies

What is a bear's favourite pasta?

Tagliateddy.

What animal cares the most about its posture?

Yoga bear.

What should you call a bald teddy?

Fred bear.

What animal do you look like when you're in the bath?

A little bear.

Why are polar bears cheap to keep?

They live on ice.

What's black and white and noisy?

A panda playing the drums.

What do you call a big white bear with a hole in his middle?

A polo bear!

What is a bear's favourite drink?

Koka-Koala.

Why was the little bear so spoiled?

Because its mother panda'd to him all the time.

Why Did the Chicken Cross the Road?

Why did the chicken cross the road?

Don't ask us, ask the chicken!

Why did the chicken run across the road?

There was a car coming.

Why did the chicken cross the road halfway?

She wanted to lay it on the line.

Why did the rubber chicken cross the road?

She wanted to stretch her legs.

Why did the Roman chicken cross the road in a rush?

She was afraid someone would Caesar.

Why did the chicken cross the road, roll in a muddy puddle and cross the road again?

Because she was a dirty double-crosser.

Why didn't the chicken skeleton cross the road?

Because she was gutless.

Why did the chicken cross the playground?

To get to the other slide.

Why did the star-struck chicken cross the road?

To see Gregory Peck.

Why did the dirty chicken cross the road?

For some fowl purpose.

Why did the rooster cross the road?

To cock-a-doodle-doo something

Why did the duck cross the road?

Because the chicken needed a day off.

Why did the chewing gum cross the road?

Because it was stuck to the chicken's foot.

Why did the dinosaur cross the road?

Because chickens hadn't evolved yet.

Why did the elephant cross the road?

To prove he wasn't chicken.

Why did the sheep cross the road?

To get to the baa-baa shop for a haircut.

Why did the cow cross the road?

To get to the udder side.

Why did the fish cross the sea?

To get to the other tide.

Why didn't the skeleton cross the road?

Because he had no body to go with.

Why did the horse cross the road?

To reach his neigh-bourhood.

Why did the donkey cross the road without looking both ways first?

Because he was an ass.

Why did the badger cross the road?
To visit his flat mate.

Why did the turtle cross the road?
To get to the Shell station.

Why did the dog cross the road?
To get to the barking lot.

Why did the fish cross the road?
To get to school.

Marry Me!

Why is marriage like a hot bath?

The longer you stay in, the colder
it gets.

A man whose house had been burgled heard that the culprit had been caught. He went straight down to the police station and demanded to speak with the burglar. The copper on duty replied, 'You'll get your chance in court, sir,' to which the man pleaded, 'Please, I just want to ask him how he got in without waking my wife. I've been trying to do that for years!'

Why is marriage like a violin?

When the sweet music's over, the strings are still attached.

How many rings do you need to be married?

An engagement ring, a wedding ring, and a suffe-ring.

Why shouldn't you marry for money?

You can borrow it for less.

When are the two times men doesn't understand women?

Before marriage and after.

At a man's funeral, the pall-bearers bump
the coffin on the church wall and hear a
moan from inside. They discover the man
is actually alive. He lives for ten more
years, and then dies. At his second funeral,
as the pall-bearers are taking the coffin
out for burial the wife cries out, 'Watch
out for the wall!'

On their fortieth wedding anniversary a sixty-year-old couple were granted two wishes by a fairy who appeared before them. The wife wished to see the world and 'poof', she had tickets for a world cruise. The husband wished for a wife thirty years younger than him and 'poof', he was ninety.

When a man picked his son up from school he asked him, 'What part did you get in the school play?' His son replied, 'I'm going to be playing a man who's been married for twenty years.' The father patted him on the back and said, 'Never mind, son, maybe next time you'll get a speaking part.'

At a medical conference, a dietician was addressing a large crowd. 'The food we eat is harmful and is slowly killing us – fast food, sugary drinks, alcohol… but there is one thing we eat that is more dangerous to our wellbeing than all of these. Does anyone know what I'm referring to?' A man in the crowd raised his hand and said, 'Wedding cake?'

Sitting at the bar, a man noticed that the bloke next to him was drinking a shot, then checking in his shirt pocket, before sipping his lager and going for another shot. This continued for about an hour before the man finally asked, 'Excuse me, mate, why do you keep checking your shirt pocket while you're drinking?' The bloke replied, 'There's a photo of my wife in there, and when she starts to look good, that's when I'm heading home.'

Did you hear about the man who muttered a few words in a church and ended up being married?

Well, he muttered a few words in his sleep a year later and wound up divorced.

A boy asked his father, 'How much does it cost to get married?' and his father replied, 'I don't know, son, I'm still paying for it.'

At a magic show, a magician performed a mind-boggling trick that wowed the crow. A woman in the audience stood up and shouted, 'How did you do that?' The magician shouted back, 'If I tell you, I'll have to kill you.' So the woman replied, 'Could you tell my husband then?'

One day a man turns to his wife and says, 'Why don't we try out different positions tonight?' The wife replies, 'Sure, you can stand by the ironing board, and I'll lie on the sofa watching TV.'

A woman goes into a gun shop and asks for a rifle. 'It's for my husband,' she informs the sales assistant. 'Did he tell you what make to get?' the assistant asks. 'Of course not!' replies the woman, 'He doesn't know I'm going to shoot him.'

A woman applied for a job at a lemon farm. Looking at her CV, the farmer said, 'I'm sorry, miss, but do you actually have any experience in picking lemons?' The woman smiled and replied, 'Well, I've been divorced three times, so I'd say I'm pretty good at it!'

The bridegroom's father patted him on the back and said, 'Congratulations. Today is the happiest day of your life – enjoy it.' The man replied, 'But dad, I'm not getting married till tomorrow.' His father said, 'I know, son. I know.'

A woman went to have her fortune read. The fortune teller stared into her crystal ball, gasped and said, 'Your husband will soon die a violent death.' Wide-eyed, the woman replied, 'Will I be acquitted?'

What's the difference between men and women when it comes to marriage?
Women worry about the future until they get married, and men never worry about the future until they do.

If love is blind, then what is marriage?
An eye-opener!

Why do nuns marry themselves to God?
Well, just think what they'd get in the divorce.

Why did Adam and Eve have such a great marriage?
He couldn't talk about his mother's cooking.

A man is standing in front of the mirror. He says to his wife, 'I've got a bit of a belly, and since we've been married I've lost all my muscle definition. And I think I might be going bald.' His wife looks up and replies, 'Well, at least there's nothing wrong with your eyes.'

While watching a medical drama, a man turned to his wife and said, 'I never want to live in a vegetative state. If that happens to me, just pull the plug.' So his wife got up, grabbed the pizza and can of lager from his hands, and pulled the plug on the TV.

The Big Roar

How does a lion greet the other animals in the field?

Pleased to eat you.

Which animal always comes top in exams?
The cheetah.

**What does the tiger say to his friends before
they go out hunting for food?**
Let us prey.

**What did the lion say to his cubs when he
taught them to hunt?**
Don't walk over the road till you see the
zebra crossing.

What does a lion brush his mane with?
A catacomb.

What's striped and bouncy?
A tiger on a pogo stick.

What happened to the leopard who took a bath three times a day?
After a week he was spotless.

On which day do lions eat people?
Chewsday.

Why did the lion feel sick after he'd eaten a priest?
Because it's hard to keep a good man down.

Burps, Barf and Bottom Behaviour

What's brown and sits in the forest?

Winnie's poo.

Two brothers are getting ready for school.
One boy is in the kitchen, having a bowl
of cornflakes, while the other is frantically
looking for his show-and-tell collection.
'I'm sure I put it in here somewhere,' he
says, before remembering he'd left it
in the kitchen. Looking on the table he
notices his brother's bowl of cereal. 'Oh, so
you found my scab collection then.'

How many men does it take to change a roll of toilet paper?

No one knows. It's never happened.

Did you hear about the American who really wanted a cent in his pocket?

He farted.

There were two flies on the toilet.

One flew away, but the other got peed off.

Did you know diarrhoea is hereditary?

Yes – it runs in your jeans!

Two men pass each other in a park. Both are dragging their right foot as they walk. One man looks at the other knowingly, points to his foot and says, 'Falklands, '82.' The other points his thumb behind him and says, 'Dog poo, ten feet that way.'

A shopkeeper greets a customer, who asks him where the toilet rolls are. 'Here you go,' says the shopkeeper. 'Did you want blue, peach, primrose yellow…?' 'White will do,' replies the man. 'I prefer to colour it myself.'

While waiting at the doctor's surgery, a man lets rip a really loud fart. Trying to look nonchalant he turns to the woman next to him as if nothing has happened. 'Do you have a copy of today's paper I could borrow?' he asks. 'No,' she replies, 'but if you put your hand out of the window you can rip some leaves off that bush.'

A famous pirate captain had a ritual that whenever battle looked imminent, he would change into his red shirt. One day his cabin boy asked him why he did this. 'It's in case I get shot,' he replied, 'I don't want my men to see the blood and get worried.' The cabin boy nodded, and then turned to see another pirate crew, sabres raised, boarding their ship. Suddenly the nervous captain said, 'Fetch me my brown trousers.'

Promising her mum that she will be back by twelve, a girl goes out to meet her friends. However, her mates persuade her to stay out longer and she doesn't get home until four in the morning. As the girl is about to climb the stairs, the grandfather clock starts to chime. She knows that her mum would have heard the front door and would be awake, so she decides to add on a few chimes of her own to make it seem as though it is midnight. In the morning, her mum remarks, 'I think we need to get someone to look at that clock. Last night it chimed four times, then there was a pause, a few strange grunting noises, and then a loud bang followed by a fart.'

Did you hear about the constipated mathematician?

He worked it out with a pencil.

Did you hear about the blind skunk?

He's dating a fart.

Why did the cantankerous old man take toilet paper to the party with him?

Because he was a party pooper.

Two flies were sitting on a dog poo. One farted and the other one turned to him and snapped, 'Do you mind? Can't you see I'm eating?'

There are three ladies in a waiting room.
The first lady compliments the second
on her perfume and asks her what it is.
'A special blend, only available in France,'
she replies haughtily. The first lady then
announces that her perfume is unique,
created just for her in a perfumery in
Egypt. They look expectantly at the
third, waiting for her contribution. She
stands up and lets out a very stinky fart.
'Cauliflower curry,' she says proudly, 'from
the Indian down the road.'

Two sisters go to visit their elderly mother in a private hospital to make sure she's receiving good care. They find that the nurses are very friendly and there is always someone around to help. For instance, every time their mother shifts in her chair, a nurse rushes over to gently straighten her up. Both daughters feel satisfied, and later ask their mother what she thinks of the place. She replies, 'Oh, it's very nice. They are very friendly and helpful here. There's only one complaint – I'm dying to do a fart, but every time I get ready to let one off they force me to suck it back up.'

Miss Brown is teaching her English class to incorporate new words into their sentences. She asks one little boy to give an example of a sentence using the word 'undoubtedly'. 'Should farts make your trousers wet and lumpy?' he asks. 'Of course not, now please just make a sentence,' answers Miss Brown. 'Well then,' replies the pupil, 'I have undoubtedly pooed my pants.'

A woman goes to see the doctor because she can't stop farting. 'It's not a huge problem because they don't smell or make a noise, but I just want them to stop. Even though you haven't noticed, I have already farted a few times in this office. Can you prescribe me something?' Looking pained, the doctor begins writing out a prescription. 'I'm prescribing some decongestants for your nose,' he says, 'and referring you for a hearing test.'

An old couple are lying in bed when the man does a big, noisy fart. 'One nil!' he exclaims gleefully. In response, the old lady rolls over and does a huge fart in his direction. 'One all!' she shouts. This carries on until the score is three apiece. It is then the old man's turn again but try as he might, he cannot fart. He tries so hard that he ends up pooing in the bed. Before his wife notices he shouts, 'Half time! Switch sides!'

A woman walks into a very expensive shoe shop to admire the display. Leaning over to pick up a particularly beautiful pair of high-heeled shoes, she accidentally lets out a fart. Seeing no one around, she thinks she has got away with it. Just then a salesman walks up to her and asks if she would like any assistance. She asks about the price of the beautiful shoes. 'Well madam,' he replies, 'if just touching them makes you fart, you are going to poo your pants when you find out how much they cost.'

At church a little girl tells her mother she's going to be sick. Her mother tells her to do it in the bushes round the back of the church. The girl leaves and comes back after about five minutes. Her mother asks her if she threw up. 'Yes,' the girl says. 'But I didn't have to go round the back, there was a little box by the front door that said, "For the Sick".'

What's the definition of bravery?

A man with diarrhoea risking a fart.

What do you call someone who doesn't fart in public?

A private tutor.

What did Mr Spock find in the toilet?

The captain's log.

Why do men whistle when they're sitting on the toilet?

Because it helps them remember which end they need to wipe.

How Many Jokes Does it Take to Change a Light Bulb?

How many amoebas does it take to change a light bulb?

One. No, two. No, four. No, eight. No, sixteen. No, thirty-two…

How many Englishmen does it take to change a light bulb?

None. I'm sure it works just fine, we've had that same light bulb for years and we've never had any problems with it.

How many academics does it take to change a light bulb?

None. That's what research students are for.

How many archaeologists does it take to change a light bulb?

Two. One to change it and another to debate with him how old the old light bulb is.

How many atheists does it take to screw in a light bulb?

None. They're never in the dark.

How many bankers does it take to change a light bulb?

One. And then he'll charge you every time you turn it on.

How many economists does it take to change a light bulb?

None. If market forces wanted the light bulb to be changed, it would've been changed already.

How many DIY enthusiasts does it take to change a light bulb?

Only one, but it takes him two full weekends and five trips to B&Q.

How many pessimists does it take to change a light bulb?

What's the point? It'll only blow again.

How many policemen does it take to screw in a light bulb?

None. It turned itself in.

How many doctors does it take to screw in a light bulb?

Only one, but he'll charge a huge fee and need a nurse to prep it for him first.

How many actors does it take to change a light bulb?

Only one. They don't like to share the spotlight.

How many admin assistants does it take to change a light bulb?

None, unless you complete a light bulb change request form before Friday.

How many medical students does it take to screw in a light bulb?

One hundred. One to change the light bulb and the other ninety-nine to stand around wondering why they weren't chosen to do it.

How many students does it take to change a light bulb?

It depends – is it part of a drinking game?

How many policemen does it take to change a light bulb?

Just one, but he is never around when you need him.

How many Mac users does it take to change a light bulb?

Only one. It doesn't matter if the new bulb doesn't work properly, as long as it's bright and shiny.

How many private school children does it take to screw in a light bulb?

None, their parents do it for them.

How many London bus drivers does it take to change a light bulb?

Sorry, we don't have change.

How many hairdressers does it take to change a light bulb?

Five. One to wash the bulb, one to colour it, one to cut it, one to dry it, and one to flit around sweeping up any broken glass.

How many divorcees does it take to change a light bulb?

None. The fixtures and fittings all went with the house.

How many PC users does it take to change a light bulb?

Two. One to restart it, and the other to throw the old one out of a window.

How many politicians does it take to change a light bulb?

The light bulb situation has been brought to the Government's attention and a select committee will be discussing how it is best to proceed in due course.

How many environmentalists does it take to change a light bulb?

One, but only if you've got solar panels on your roof.

How many movie stars does it take to change a light bulb?

One, but he only takes one step up the ladder and then his stunt double takes over.

How many shop assistants does it take to change a light bulb?

One, but they'll only change it if the old one's in the exact condition you bought it in and you have the receipt.

How many managers does it take to change a light bulb?

Only one to justify exactly why it's not their responsibility and call a subordinate to change it for them.

How many ASBO teenagers does it take to change a light bulb?

One, but check your pockets and the rest of your house for any missing valuables.

How many modern artists does it take to change a light bulb?

None. It's not supposed to be changed – it's art!

How many men does it take to change a light bulb?

Only one, but you'll have to nag him for a month first.

How many real men does it take to change a light bulb?

None. Real men aren't afraid of the dark.

How many computer software engineers does it take to change a light bulb?

None. They just let the marketing team explain that 'darkness' is a new, special feature.

How many mechanics does it take to change a light bulb?

We don't know yet. They're still waiting on a part.

How many Australians does it take to change a light bulb?

Two. One to say, 'No worries, mate!' and one to fetch the beers.

How many teenagers does it take to change a light bulb?

It depends, how many bribes are involved?

How many lawyers does it take to change a light bulb?

How many can you afford?

Fly Away Birdie

What's red and green and jumps out of aeroplanes?

A parrot-trooper.

Which birds spend all their time on their knees?
Birds of prey.

When is the best time to buy a budgie?
When they're going cheep.

Where do birds meet for coffee?
In a nest-cafe.

How does a bird with a broken wing manage to land safely?
With it's sparrowchute.

Which bird is always out of breath?
A puffin.

Where do parrots get their qualifications?
At a polytechnic.

What do you give a sick bird?
Tweetment.

What do owls say when it is raining?
Too wet to woo!

What kind of bird tastes fruity?
A kiwi.

How do you get a baby swan's autograph?
Ask for its cygnet-ure.

Why do ducks watch the news?

For the feather forecast.

What kind of birds go on strike?

Mynah birds.

How do you know that owls are smarter than chickens?

Have you ever heard of Kentucky Fried Owl?

Which birds steal soap from the bath?

Robber ducks.

Where do birds invest their money?

In the stork market.

What happens when ducks fly upside down?

They quack up.

What did they call the canary that flew into the pastry dish?

Tweetie Pie.

What kind of birds do you usually find locked up?

Jailbirds.

What happened when the owl lost his voice?

He didn't give a hoot.

Seagulls fly over the sea, but what flies over the bay?

Bagels.

Wicket Wisecracks

Why did Robin get sent off the field?

Because he broke his bat, man.

Two cricket team mates were having a pint. One said to the other, 'What's up? You're looking miserable.' The other replied, 'I am. My doctor told me I can't play cricket.' His friend looked surprised and said, 'I didn't know he was at the game on Sunday.'

Two cricket fans were discussing a recent court case. 'So, he was a hit and run driver, then?' asked the first. 'Yes,' said his friend, 'I hear he's batting for the prison cricket team this season.'

What did the cricketer say when the journalist asked him to explain his poor batting average?

I'm stumped.

Why did the American spectator cry when his team's bowler hit the stumps?

Because he thought he was aiming for the bat.

Why do most cricketers look weather-beaten?

Because rain always stops play.

A new cricket umpire was learning the ropes. He asked his trainer, 'Do I have to run after the ball?' His trainer replied, 'No, just after the match.'

A batsman dismissed from the field passed the man in the white coat and snapped, 'You need glasses.' The man replied, 'So do you, mate. I'm just selling burgers.'

The Devil suggested there should be a cricket match between heaven and hell. 'That wouldn't work,' said God, smiling. 'We have all the cricketers.' The Devil replied, 'Yes, but we have all the umpires.'

Batsman: My wife said she's going to leave me if I don't stop playing cricket.

Wicket keeper: Oh dear. That's terrible.

Batsman: Yes, I suppose I'll miss her.

Brian asked his boss for the afternoon off so he could go to his uncle's funeral. He actually went to a cricket match where the score was 220 for 0. Turning around he came face-to-face with his boss. 'So, I suppose this is your uncle's funeral,' said his boss, rather annoyed. 'Could be,' replied Brian. 'He's the bowler.'

The batsman collapsed in a miserable heap in the pavilion and moaned, 'I've never played that badly before. I don't know what happened.' His captain turned around and replied, 'Oh, you've played before, have you?'

Why is it called a hat-trick?

Because it's performed by a bowler.

Middlesex and Yorkshire were playing at Lords. A man with a large white rose approached the ticket office and asked the price. 'Ten pounds please, sir,' was the girl's reply. 'Well then, there's five pounds,' the man said, handing over the money. 'There's only one team worth watching.'

Doctor, doctor, I feel like a cricket ball.

You'll soon be over that.

Doctor, doctor, every time I use my cricket bat I feel like crying.

Perhaps it's a weeping willow.

After a bad day's play, the cricketer who had dropped six catches was getting dressed in the changing rooms. Sniffling, he said, 'I think I've caught a cold.' His captain, who was changing nearby replied, 'Thank goodness you can catch something.'

It's a Funny Old Thing

What should you do if you want to see less wrinkles?

Take off your glasses.

Two elderly ladies were planning their outfits for the country club dinner dance. 'We're supposed to wear something that matches our husband's hair, so I'm wearing a white silk trouser suit,' said one lady. 'Oh,' said the other, 'I better not go then.'

An elderly man was driving down the M5 when his mobile rang. Answering, he heard his wife's voice saying, 'Darling, be careful, on the news it says there's a car driving the wrong way down the M5.' To which he replied, 'It's not just one car, it's all of them!'

Three elderly gentlemen were taking a walk in the park. One remarked to the other, 'Windy, ain't it?' to which his friend replied, 'No, it's Thursday.' The third man said: 'So am I. Let's go and get a cup of tea.'

On a crowded bus, one man noticed that the man next to him had his eyes closed. 'Are you OK?' he asked. 'Yeah, I'm fine,' was the gentleman's reply, 'I just hate to see old ladies standing.'

Two old men are sitting in the garden, when one turns to the other and says, 'I'm eighty-six years old and I'm full of aches and pains. You're about my age – how do you feel?' The other man answers back, 'I feel just like a newborn baby.' Shocked, the first man asks, 'Really? How come?' to which his friend replies, 'No hair, no teeth and I think I've just wet my pants.'

One elderly man says to another, 'I just bought a great state-of-the-art hearing aid – it cost me a fortune!' The other man asks, 'Really, what kind is it?' to which the first man replies, 'Four thirty.'

An old man's wife whispers to him, 'Let's go upstairs and make passionate love.' The old man considers for a moment and then replies, 'Darling, I can't do both.'

Why are an old man's wife and his teeth so similar?

He doesn't sleep with either.

What's the best thing about being elderly and on holiday?

Your energy runs out before your money does.

When do old people feel lucky?

When they find their car in the car park.

Three elderly ladies were talking about the trials of old age. 'Sometimes when I'm holding something in the kitchen I can't remember if I'm getting it out or putting it away,' one lady said. 'Me too,' chimed in another, 'When I'm on the landing I don't always know if I'm going up or going down.' Then the third lady said, 'Oh dear, I'm so lucky I still have all my marbles, touch wood.' She knocked on the coffee table and then said, 'Oh, that must be the door – I'll get it.'

At her husband's funeral the undertaker approached the widow. 'How old was your husband?' he asked. 'He was ninety-seven – two years older than me.' 'So you're ninety-five, then,' surmised the undertaker. 'Hardly worth going home, really.'

'I love your alligator shoes!' says one elderly man to another. The man replies, 'I'm not wearing any shoes.'

Furry Friends

Which European city has the largest rodent population?

Hamsterdam.

What are female mice better at than male mice?

Mousework.

What kind of musical instruments do mice play?

Mouse organs.

What has large antlers, a high voice and wears white gloves?

Mickey Moose.

Why do mice need oiling?

Because they squeak.

Who do you call if you need a rodent-crime solving?

Miami Mice.

What has twelve legs, three tails and can't see?

Three blind mice.

What do you get when you pour boiling water down a rabbit hole?

Hot cross bunnies.

What is small, furry and smells like bacon?

A hamster.

What are small, crisp and squeaky when you eat them?

Mice Krispies.

What is small, furry and brilliant at fencing?

A mouseketeer.

What's grey, squeaky and hangs around in caves?

Stalagmice.

What was the Energizer Bunny arrested for?

Battery.

What's the hardest part of milking a mouse?

Stopping it from falling in the bucket.

What's grey and furry on the inside and white on the outside?

A mouse sandwich.

What do mice do when they move into a new home?

Throw a mouse-warming party.

What is a mouse's favourite game?

Hide and squeak.

A Man Walks Into a Bar...

A man walks into a bar with a slab of tarmac under his arm and says, 'A beer please, and one for the road.'

A man walks into a bar. The bartender
chucks him out because he's too drunk.
Then the drunk walks back into the bar,
so the bartender ejects him again. Seconds
later the drunk walks back into the bar,
and just as the bartender is throwing him
out of the door again the drunk slurs,
'How many bars do you own anyway?'

A man walks into a bar. The bartender says, 'See those two beef sirloins nailed to the ceiling? Here's a dart. If you hit one, you get to take them home and your drinks are on the house.' The man replies, 'No thanks, the steaks are too high.'

An Englishman, an Irishman and a Scotsman walk into a bar. The bartender says, 'What is this? Some kind of joke?'

A brain goes into a bar and orders a pint of beer. The barman says, 'I'm not serving you, you're out of your skull!'

Charles Dickens walks into a bar and asks for a Martini. The bartender replies, 'Olive or twist?'

A neutron walks into a bar and orders a beer. The bartender sets the beer down and says, 'For you, no charge!'

A Shetland pony walks into a bar and says, 'Can I have an orange juice, please?' The bartender leans forward and asks, 'What was that?' 'An orange juice,' tries the pony again. 'You'll have to speak up, sir!' exclaims the bartender. 'I'm sorry,' says the pony, 'I'm just a little hoarse.'

An irate pirate swaggers into a bar with a wooden ship's steering wheel hanging from his belt. The bartender asks, 'What's that for?' The pirate responds, 'Aarrr, it's drivin' me nuts.'

A horse trots into a bar. The bartender says, 'Cheer up, mate, why the long face?'

A piece of rope walks into a bar. 'We don't serve your kind in here,' the bartender says, throwing him out. The rope goes outside, ties himself in a knot and frays one of his ends. He goes back into the bar. 'Weren't you just in here?' says the bartender. 'No,' the rope replies, 'I'm a frayed knot.'

A man walks into his local and sees a tiger pulling pints. 'What are you staring at?' growls the tiger. 'Haven't you ever seen a tiger serving drinks before?' 'Sorry, it's not that,' replies the man. 'I just never thought the lions would sell this place.'

William Shakespeare walks into a bar and asks for a white wine spritzer. 'I can't serve you,' says the bartender. 'You're Bard!'

A pig goes into a bar and orders ten beers. When he gets up to leave the bartender says, 'Do you want me to show you where the toilets are?' The pig squeals, 'Nah, I'll go wee wee wee all the way home.'

A hotdog walks into a bar. The bartender says, 'Sorry, we don't serve food in here.'

A grasshopper hops into a bar. The bartender says, 'Wow, what an honour. What's it like having a drink named after you?' The grasshopper looks shocked and says, 'What, you've got a drink named Dave?'

A goldfish flops into a bar and looks at the bartender. The bartender asks, 'What can I get you?' The goldfish says, 'Water.'

A man walks into a pub and sits down next to a dog. The man asks the landlord, 'Does your dog bite?' 'Never!' the landlord replies. So the man reaches down to pet the dog and the dog bites him. 'I thought you said your dog doesn't bite!' the man exclaims. 'He doesn't,' the landlord retorts. 'That isn't my dog.'

A cowboy walks out of a bar and notices someone has painted his horse. Strolling back in he yells, 'Which one of you painted my horse?' A large, tattooed fellow rises. 'It was me,' he says, preparing his fists for a fight. Realising he's in trouble, the cowboy tips his hat and says, 'Thank you, sir, just wanted to let you know the first coat's dry!'

What did the man say when he walked into the bar?
Ouch!

An amnesiac walks into a bar. He asks, 'Excuse me, do I come here often?'

A man walks into a bar clutching a set of jump leads. The bartender says, 'You can come in, just don't start anything!'

A man walks into a bar holding a pot-bellied pig in one hand and a duck in the other. 'I'll have a whisky,' he says to the bartender. 'And I'll have a G and T,' says the pig. The startled bartender gasps and says, 'Wow, that's amazing, I've never seen a talking pig before.' 'He can't talk,' declares the man. 'The duck is a ventriloquist.'

A man walks into a bar with a gerbil on his head. The bartender asks, 'Can I help you, sir?' 'Yeah,' the gerbil says, 'you can get this man off my bum!'

Two men walk into a bar, the third one ducks.

A man walks into a bar carrying a newt. 'What's his name?' asks the bartender. 'I call him Shorty,' replies the man, 'because he's my newt!'

A gremlin walks into a bar, orders a pint and plops down next to a local. After half his drink the gremlin leans over and sticks his head in the man's beer. The man says nothing, and the evening continues. The gremlin does this nine more times as he continues to drink beer after beer. On the tenth time the man grabs the gremlin and says, 'Put your head in my beer one more time and I'll pull your penis off.' 'You can't,' says the gremlin. 'I haven't got one.' Confused, the man says, 'Well, how do you go to the toilet?' 'Like this,' says the gremlin, dunking his head into the man's beer.

A woman went into a bar and asked for a 'double entendre'. So the bartender gave her one.

A zebra walks into a bar and orders a beer. The bartender says, 'That'll be £5. We don't get many zebras in here, you know.' The zebra pays the bartender and replies, 'Well, at £5 a beer, I can see why!'

A man sits down at a bar and hears someone say, 'You look hot today.' A few minutes later he hears the same small voice: 'Your hair's looking great!' The man asks the bartender, 'Who said that?' 'That'll be the peanuts,' says the bartender. 'They're complimentary!'

Two bottles of probiotic yogurt walk into a bar. The bartender says to them, 'Get out, we don't serve your kind here.' 'Why not?!' screams one of the bottles. 'We're cultured individuals.'

Nine-to-Five Nonsense

Why did all the staff at the paper company lose their jobs?

Because the company folded.

A rookie executive was heading home late when he spotted the CEO in the photocopy room holding a piece of paper next to the shredder. The CEO looked confused so, seeing his chance to win favour, the young executive offered to help. 'This is a very important document,' said the CEO. 'My secretary's left for the night, and I can't get this thing to work.' 'No problem,' said the young worker. He took the piece of paper, turned on the shredder, and inserted the document. 'You got it working! Fantastic!' said the CEO excitedly. 'Now can I have three copies?'

Which sea creature's job is it to keep the ocean clean?

A mermaid.

What did the electrician's wife say when her husband didn't come home on time?

Wire you insulate?

Did you hear about the blind carpenter who picked up his hammer and saw?

You can tell a British builder by his hands – they're always in his pockets.

If you're an optimist, the glass is half full.
If you're a pessimist, the glass is half empty.
**And if you're an engineer, the glass is two
times bigger than it needs to be.**

**There was a secretary who lost all her fingers
in a snowboarding accident.**
The company kept her on to take shorthand.

There was a nasty smell in the office, so one girl said, 'Please will someone do something about their deodorant – it obviously isn't working.' The bloke sitting next to her swung round and announced, 'Well, it can't be mine because I'm not wearing any.'

A painter was hired to paint a row of houses. On the first day he painted five houses, on the second he managed two houses, and on the third day he only managed half a house. His boss took him aside and asked, 'Why are you doing less work each day?' The worker replied, 'Because every day I am getting further away from the paint can.'

At a job interview the employer asked the applicant, 'It says on your CV you've been at your current job for twenty-five years, but you're only twenty-seven years old. How can that be?' The applicant replied, 'Well, I did a lot of overtime.'

Funny Felines

What happened to the cat that ate a ball of wool?

She had mittens.

What do cat actors say on stage?
Tabby or not tabby.

What did the cat say when he lost all his money?
I'm paw.

How do you know if your cat has a throat infection?
It has cat-arrh.

What do you do with a blue Burmese?
Try and cheer it up a bit.

How is cat food sold?

Usually purr can.

What is a cat's favourite cereal?

Shredded Tweet.

Why did the cat join the Red Cross?

Because it wanted to be a first-aid kit.

Who was the most powerful cat in China?

Chairman Miaow.

What is cleverer than a talking cat?

A spelling bee.

What is white, sugary, has whiskers and floats on the sea?

A catameringue.

What is a crazy marmalade cat's favourite biscuit?

A ginger nut.

Why do cats chase birds?

For a lark.

Where do cats get their information?

Mewspapers.

What happened when the cat swallowed a coin?

There was some money in the kitty.

What works in a circus, walks a tightrope and has claws?

An acrocat.

Why did the cat eat some cheese?

So he could wait by the mouse hole with baited breath.

Laugh-in-laws

What's the difference between outlaws and in-laws?

Outlaws are wanted.

A man takes his dog to the vet and asks him to cut the dog's tail off. Examining the healthy wagging tail the vet says, 'But why would you want me to do that? This tail is fine.' The man replies, 'My mother-in-law is coming to stay for a week and I don't want anything in our house to make her feel like she's welcome.'

What's the worst thing a doctor can tell you after your mother-in-law has been in an accident and taken to A&E?

Don't worry – she's going to make it.

What should you do if you find your mother-in-law stuck in concrete up to her waist?

Get more concrete.

What do mothers-in-law call their kitchen brooms?

Basic transportation.

A woman's husband went missing, so she spoke to the police and gave them some photos of him. 'Is there anything you'd like us to say to your husband if we locate him?' asked the officer. The woman replied, 'Just tell him my mother changed her mind, she's not coming this weekend.'

A British man was on a religious pilgrimage to Jerusalem with his wife, children and their grandparents when his mother-in-law became sick and died. He went to the British consulate to find out about returning the body back to England. 'It will cost £5,000 to return the body, but you could bury her here for £150,' said the consul. 'No,' said the man, 'I'd like to bring her back to England.' The consul replied, 'Considering the price difference, you must have loved your mother-in-law very much.' 'No,' said the man again, 'It's just there's a history of resurrection in this town, and I don't want to take any chances.'

A man was late home from work, so his wife called her mother. 'I'm sure he's having an affair,' said the wife. 'Why do you always assume the worst?' asked her mother. 'Maybe he's just been in a car accident.'

Two men are drinking in a pub. One says to the other, 'My mother-in-law is an angel.'
His friend replies, 'You're lucky, mate, mine's still alive.'

A door-to-door fundraiser was greeted at one house by a man. 'Hello, sir, would you like to donate anything to the local old people's home?' asked the fundraiser. The man replied, 'Yes, please – my mother-in-law.'

On the beach a man sees a woman drowning far away in the sea. He calls to the lifeguard passing by, 'Help! My wife is drowning. I can't swim, but if you save her I'll give you one hundred pounds.' Immediately the lifeguard dives into the water, swims to the woman and pulls her safely to shore. Exhausted he asks the husband, 'Where's my one hundred pounds?' 'I'm sorry, mate,' says the husband. 'From a distance I thought this lady was my wife, but it's my mother-in-law.' The lifeguard shrugs his shoulders and says, 'Just my luck. How much do I owe you?'

Doctor: I'm sorry to tell you that your mother-in-law has suffered a heart attack.

Son-in-law: Sorry, doctor, but that's impossible.

Doctor: What do you mean?

Son-in-law: It's just, she doesn't have a heart.

A woman asked her son-in-law, 'If you hate me so much why do you insist I come on holidays with you?' He replied, 'It's so I don't have to kiss you goodbye.'

A man tells his mate that he is buying his mother-in-law a jaguar. 'But I thought you didn't like her,' says his friend. 'I know what I'm doing,' says the man. 'That thing's bitten her three times today already!'

A man asks his brother, 'What's your idea of a perfect morning?' His sibling replies, 'Waking up and seeing my mother-in-law's face on a milk carton.'

After proposing to his girlfriend a man invited his mother round for dinner to meet her. When his mother arrived she was greeted by her son and three women – a blonde, a brunette and a redhead. She asked her son why there were three women, and he explained that he wanted to see if she could guess which lady was her future daughter-in-law. The mother looked at each girl carefully and then answered, 'It's the redhead.' Her son was shocked. 'How could you tell so quickly?' he asked. His mother replied, 'Because I can't stand her.'

A woman comes home to find her mother standing in a bucket of water with her fingers in a plug socket. Her husband is standing next to her mother with his finger on the switch. 'Hello, darling,' says her mother. 'Your wonderful husband has come up with a fantastic way to cure my arthritis.'

A woman saw a funeral procession coming up the road. Following the two hearses was a woman with a dog, and behind her some 200 women walking in single file. This was too bizarre to ignore so she approached the woman with the dog and asked, 'Excuse me, I'm sorry for your loss, but who is this funeral procession for?' The woman replied, 'The first hearse is for my husband; he was killed by our dog. The second is for my mother-in-law; the dog killed her when she tried to help her son.' 'That's terrible,' the first woman said, and then after some thought she asked, 'Can I borrow your dog?' The second woman pointed to the line of women and said, 'Join the queue.'

Two cannibals are sitting around the barbeque eating. One says to the other, 'I really can't stand my mother-in-law.' The other replies, 'No worries, there's plenty of salad and mashed potatoes.'

A man asks his friend, 'What two things about your mother-in-law do you hate the most?' His mate replies, 'Her chins.'

A genie appears before a man and grants him two wishes. The genie says to wish carefully, because whatever the man wishes for, the same wish will be doubled and granted to his mother-in-law. After some thought the man says, 'I wish for one million pounds, and to be beaten half to death.'

A man was found guilty of bigamy. At his sentencing the judge asked, 'Have you learned why it's bad to have three wives?' The man replied, 'Yes, your honour. Three wives means three mothers-in-law, and that could lead a lesser man to suicide.'

A man and his mother-in-law lived happily for 30 years.

Then they met each other.

A woman was in a house fire and needed a skin graft for her face. Because she was so thin, the doctor said that her only option was for someone to donate skin. Her husband was a match, but only the skin from his buttocks was suitable, so they both agreed to keep it a secret and the operation went ahead. Afterwards, the woman looked more beautiful than she had ever looked before. One day, she was home with her husband and said, 'Darling, how can I ever thank you for what you did for me?' He replied, 'There's no need – I get all the thanks I need every time I see your mum kiss you on the cheek!'

Hearing of King Soloman's wise decisions, two fighting mothers dragged a young gentleman before the sovereign. 'This man promised to marry my daughter,' said the first woman. 'No, he agreed to marry mine,' argued the second. King Solomon puzzled over this problem and concluded, 'I shall settle this by sawing the young man in two, and both your daughters will receive one half of him.' 'Sounds good to me,' said the first woman. 'No!' cried the second, 'Her daughter can marry him.' 'Ah ha!' said wise Solomon. 'The man must marry the first woman's daughter, because she was the only one willing to see him cut in half – she is the true mother-in-law!'

Pirate Leg-pullers

What designer brand do pirates love?

Arrrrrmani.

Why do little pirates struggle with the alphabet?

Because they think there are seven 'C's.

Why didn't the pirate drink rum?

Because he was on the port side.

One pirate said to another, 'That be a fine looking hook and peg-leg ye got there.' The other replied, 'Well I should hope so – they cost me an arm and a leg!'

Where do pirates shop for shoes?

Clarrrrrks.

Why can you never reach a pirate on the phone?
Because they leave it off the hook.

What has eight arms and eight legs?
Eight pirates.

What do pirates love to dance to?
Arrrrr and B.

What do pirates love most about birthday parties?
Da-balloons.

Did you hear about the pirate who got a great deal on a new ship?
It was on sail.

Why did the pirate have a big bottom?

He kept stealing people's booty.

What did the pirate say when it was time for lunch?

I'm starrrrrving!

What do pirates say when they have a heart attack?

'Arrrrr! Me heartie!'

Why did the pirate make everyone bow?

Because he was being very stern.

Have you heard about the new scary pirate movie?

It's rated arrrrrgh!

What vegetable do pirates always eat?

Arrrrrtichokes.

Why should you never fight a pirate?

They've all got mean right hooks.

Where does a pirate keep his cows?

In his barnacle.

Where do pirates keep their valuables?

Davy Jones' Locker.

Why didn't the pirate starve on the desert island?

Because of all the sand which is there.

How do pirates pass wind?

They farrrrrt.

What did the pirate want to be when he grew up?

An arrrrrchitect.

Why was the pirate's daughter sad?

She had a sunken chest.

Why do pirates have addictive personalities?

Because once ye lose yer first hand, ye get hooked.

What's a pirate's favourite action movie?

Arrrrmageddon.

Frolics on the Fairway

Why did the golfer always wear two pairs of trousers?

In case he got a hole in one.

Why are new clubs better than old cars?

You can drive further with new clubs.

Why did the golfer's wife ask to be buried on the golf course?

So she could be sure her husband would visit her grave.

Doctor, doctor, I think I'm a golf ball.

Well, you've come a fair way to see me.

What's the difference between 'put' and 'putt'?

'Put' means to place something where you want it, and 'putt' is a vain attempt at the same thing.

While hanging out in the clubhouse a golfer says to his friend, 'Did I tell you I got a great new set of golf clubs for my wife?' The friend replies, 'Wow, that was a good deal!'

Lucy sent her tee shot all the way down the fairway and straight into the hole. Her delight only faded when Robert said, 'Right, one more practice shot each and we'll start for real.'

Ernie played golf with his mates every weekend, even though he was a truly awful player. Finally, one day, his friends asked him, 'Ernie, why do you like golf so much when you're so bad?' Ernie replied, 'I don't like golf. I'm just here to get away from my wife – I thought that's what we were all doing!'

Why shouldn't you hit your caddie with your putter?

Because you can hit him harder with a driver.

How should you stop rabbits digging up the fairway?

Hide their spades.

What's the difference between a grumpy golfer and a cheerful golfer?

Roughly twenty-five strokes.

How do golfers die?

They just putter out.

A golfer hits his ball into a water hazard and wonders whether to wade in to get it. He asks an old man nearby how deep the lake is. The man replies, 'An inch or so.' The golfer steps off the edge and disappears underwater. 'Strange,' mutters the old man. 'It only goes part way up those ducks.'

Wife: You think about golf more than you think about me. Do you even remember the day we got married?

Husband: How could I forget it? I drove 280 yards from the sixth that very morning!

Golfer: I would move the whole of heaven and the entire earth to break par on this hole.

Caddie: I'd recommend heaven, sir. You couldn't move any more earth if you tried.

TV interviewer: Would you say St Andrews is the most difficult course in the world?

Golfer: St Andrews is the most difficult course in the world.

John and Charlie were playing golf in the Antarctic, when they saw a man fishing through the ice. 'Who'd be fishing in these conditions?' guffawed Charlie.

Golfer: How do you think I could improve my game?

Caddie: Have a break from it for a couple of weeks, sir.

Golfer: Good idea. Then what?

Caddie: Take up cricket.

Two earwigs lived in the rough on the seventh hole.

First earwig: There's a man swinging a club around above us – I think he's going to squash us!

Second earwig: Hop onto that round white thing, it's the only thing he hasn't hit yet.

Why is a poor golfer like an old car?

They both go 'putt, putt, putt'.

What does a golfing fanatic's child call his father?

Par.

Why are golf clubs like reality?

You start to lose your grip on them as you get older.

What happened to the golfer whose tee shot went through the clubhouse window?

He was arrested for dangerous driving.

What Do You Get if You Cross...

What do you get if you cross a lemon with a cat?

A sourpuss.

What do you get if you cross an abbot with a trout?

Monkfish.

What do you get if you cross a zebra with a needle?

Pinstripes.

What do you get if you cross an elephant with a rhino?

El-if-i-no.

What do you get if you cross a bell with a chicken?

An alarm cluck.

What do you get if you cross a dog with a rose?

A collie-flower.

What do you get if you cross a cow with a camel?

Lumpy milkshakes.

What do you get if you cross a snake with a Lego set?

A boa constructor.

What do you get if you cross a computer with a potato?

Microchips.

What do you get if you cross an aerobics class with apple pie?

Puff pastry.

What do you get if you cross a teacher with a vampire?

Blood tests.

What do you get if you cross a hare with the bagpipes?

Hopscotch.

What do you get if you cross a cow with a mule?

Milk with a kick to it.

What do you get if you cross a motorway with a skateboard?

Run over.

What do you get if you cross a teddy bear with a pig?

A teddy boar.

What do you get if you cross a skunk with an owl?

A smelly bird that doesn't give a hoot.

What do you get if you cross a frog with some mist?

Kermit the Fog.

What do you get if you cross a kangaroo with a mink?

A fur coat with pockets.

What do you get if you cross a tomcat with a Pekingese?

A Peking tom.

What do you get if you cross a grizzly bear with a harp?

A bear-faced lyre.

What do you get if you cross a pineapple with a zipper?

A fruit fly.

What do you get if you cross an orange with a comedian?

Peels of laughter.

What do you get if you cross an elephant with a kangaroo?

Big holes all over Australia.

What do you get if you cross a dog with a telephone?

A golden receiver.

What do you get if you cross a duck with a firework?

A firequacker.

What do you get if you cross a snake with shortcrust pastry?

A pie-thon.

What do you get if you cross a Mars Bar with an elk?

Chocolate moose.

What do you get if you cross a parrot with a centipede?

A walkie-talkie.

What do you get if you cross a cow, a sheep and a goat?

The Milkybaa kid.

What do you get if you cross a duck with a steamroller?

A flat duck.

What do you get if you cross a baby deer with a hornet?

Bambee.

What do you get if you cross ham with a karate expert?

Pork chops.

What do you get if you cross a hedgehog with a boa constrictor?

A few feet of barbed wire.

What do you get if you cross fishing with a rabbit?

A hare net.

What do you get if you cross Mary Poppins with an owl?

A hootenanny.

What do you get if you cross a glow-worm with some beer?

Light ale.

What do you get if you cross a doorbell with a hummingbird?

A humdinger.

What do you get if you cross a parrot with a shark?

A bird that will talk your ear off.

What do you get if you cross a banana with a silky red dress?

A pink slip.

What do you get if you cross a canary with a mole?

A miner bird.

What do you get if you cross an artist with a policeman?

A brush with the law.

What do you get if you cross some ants with some tics?

All sorts of antics.

What do you get if you cross a sheep with a kangaroo?

A woolly jumper.

What do you get if you cross a parrot with a woodpecker?

A bird that talks in Morse code.

What do you get if you cross a cactus with a pig?

A porkerpine.

What do you get if you cross a policeman with a telegram?

Copper wire.

What do you get if you cross a zebra with a kangaroo?

A stripey jumper.

What do you get if you cross a salmon, a bird's leg and a hand?

Bird's thigh fish fingers.

What do you get if you cross a pig with an Eskimo?

A polar boar.

Waggy Dog Tales

What dog loves to take bubble baths?

A shampoodle.

What is the only kind of dog that you can eat?

A hot dog.

What kind of dogs do vampires own as pets?

Bloodhounds.

What is a dog's favourite city?

New Yorkie.

Who is a dog's favourite comedian?

Growlcho Marx.

Why are dogs so good at finding their way around?

Because they're great at dog-raphy.

What do you get if you take a really big dog out for a walk?

A Great Dane out.

What do lady dogs wear under their skirts?

Petticoats.

What happened to the dog that ate nothing but garlic?

His bark was much worse than his bite.

What did the hungry Dalmatian say after eating?

'That hit the spots.'

Which dog needs contact lenses?

A cock-eyed spaniel.

Why is it called a 'litter' of puppies?

Because they mess up the whole house.

What kind of dog chases anything red?

A bull dog.

Why do dogs run in circles?

Because it's hard to run in squares.

What do baby dogs eat at the cinema?

Pupcorn.

How did the little Scottish dog feel when he saw the Loch Ness Monster?

Terrier-fied.

How do you find your dog if he's lost in the woods?

Put your ear to a tree and listen for the bark.

How do you keep a dog from barking in your front garden?

Put him in your back garden.

If you take your dog into town, where should you leave him?

In a barking lot.

What did the dog do when a man-eating tiger followed him?

Nothing. It was a man-eating tiger, not a dog-eating one.

What place of business helps dogs that have lost their tails?

A retail store.

Which dog can tell time?

A watchdog.

Why did the dog sleep on the chandelier?

He was a light sleeper.

The Law of Laughter

What do you get when you pour cement on a burglar?

A hardened criminal.

A man was in a hurry to get his son to a doctor's appointment on time. After taking a wrong turn he made an illegal U-turn. 'Whoops!' he said to his son, 'I don't think I should've made that turn.' His son looked out of the back window and said, 'I think it's OK, dad, the police car driving behind us just did the same thing.'

A pastry chef was found dead covered in whipped cream and cherries.

The police are saying he topped himself.

A policeman was called out to a fancy dress party by disgruntled neighbours. He arrested a man dressed as a robber, who later turned out to be a High Court judge. Well you know what they say: you should never book a judge by his cover.

A policeman was out on patrol when he saw
a woman knitting while driving. 'Pull over!' he
shouted out of his car window. 'No officer,' she
replied. 'It's a hat!'

**Policeman: I'm going to have to ask you to
put your dog on a lead – it was chasing that
man on a bicycle.**
Dog walker: That's ridiculous, Rex can't even ride
a bike.

A police officer tries to pull a man over for speeding, but the driver speeds up. A chase ensues, but eventually the driver gives up and pulls over. The policeman tells the driver he's about to finish his shift, and if the man can give him a really good reason for his speeding behaviour then he'll let him go. The man replies, 'My wife ran off with a copper last week, and I thought you might be him trying to give her back.'

Two men were robbing a block of flats when they heard sirens approaching. The first man said, 'I can hear the cops coming – jump!' His thieving buddy screeched, 'But we're on the thirteenth floor!' The first man grabbed his partner and replied, 'Get a grip – this is no time to be superstitious!'

A shipment of expensive soaps were stolen from the dockyard.

Police say the thieves made a clean getaway.

A policeman pulled over an erratic driver and was surprised when the man fell out of the car. 'You're drunk!' he declared, shocked by the man's state. 'Thank goodness for that,' slurred the driver. 'I thought the steering had gone!'

A woman was pulled over for driving too fast. When the officer said, 'Why were you speeding?' the woman replied, 'I wanted to make it home before I felt really drunk.'

A policeman starts crying after he pulls over a motorist. 'Why are you upset?' says the driver. The policeman replies, 'It was a moving violation.'

Policeman: I'm afraid I'll have to lock you up for the night.
Man: Oh really? What's the charge?
Policeman: Oh, there's no charge. It's all part of the service.

Did you hear about the police station that had its toilets stolen?

The coppers had nothing to go on.

Did you hear about the woman whose wig was stolen?

The police are combing the area.

What's the difference between a dead lawyer on the road and a dead cat on the road?

There are skid marks in front of the cat.

Why are lawyers buried 18 feet under rather than just 6 feet under?

Because deep, deep down they're good people.

What do you call a clairvoyant midget who's on the run from the police?

A small medium at large.

How many coppers does it take to push a man down a flight of stairs?

None. He fell.

What did the robber say to the lady who caught him stealing her silver?

'I'm at your service, madam.'

Why did the burglar cut the legs off his bed?

He wanted to lie low for a while.

'Get this,' said a bloke to his mates. 'Last night while I was out with you lot, there was a break-in at my house.' 'Did the burglar leave with anything?' his mates asked. 'Yeah – a broken jaw, a cracked rib and two black eyes. The missus thought it was me coming home drunk.'

A flustered bank robber ran into a bank,
pointed a banana at one of the cashiers
and shouted, 'This is a muck-up!'
'Don't you mean a stick-up?' asked
the cashier.
'No,' said the robber, 'it's definitely a
muck-up. I forgot my gun!'

A policeman was escorting a man he'd arrested to the station when his hat fell off and rolled away. 'Would you like me to get that for you?' asked the considerate arrestee.

'I wasn't born yesterday,' said the officer. 'You stay here and I'll get it.'

Why was the fountain pen sent to prison?

To do a long sentence.

What type of burglary is not dangerous?

A safe robbery.

What did the burglar say to the watchmaker as he stole from his shop?

Sorry to take so much of your valuable time.

Who is the biggest gangster in the ocean?

Al Caprawn.

An Elephant Never Forgets

What goes up slowly and comes down quickly?

An elephant in a lift.

What did the tourists say when they saw a herd of elephants running over the hill wearing sunglasses and fake moustaches?

Nothing. They didn't recognise them.

Why did the elephant paint his toenails red?

So he could hide in the cherry tree.

How do you know when there is an elephant under your bed?

When your nose touches the ceiling.

How does an elephant get down from a tree?

He sits on a leaf and waits till autumn.

Why were the elephants thrown out of the swimming pool?

Because they couldn't hold their trunks up.

What's grey and never needs ironing?

A drip-dry elephant.

What's grey and goes round and round?

An elephant in a washing machine.

What's yellow on the outside and grey on the inside?

An elephant disguised as a banana.

What's big and grey and has sixteen wheels?

An elephant on roller skates.

What weighs four tons and is bright red?

An elephant holding its breath.

What has three tails, four trunks and six feet?

An elephant with spare parts.

What's grey, beautiful and wears glass slippers?

Cinderelephant.

Why are elephants grey?

So you can tell them from flamingos.

**What do elephants do when they
can't sleep?**

They take trunkquilisers.

**What did the grape say when the elephant
stood on it?**

Nothing, it just let out a little wine.

**Have you heard about the elephant that
went on a crash diet?**

He ran into three cars, a bus and two fire engines.

Why do elephants do well in school?
Because they have a lot of grey matter.

Which animals were last to board the ark?
The elephants, because their trunks had to go
through security.

What do elephants do in the evenings?
Watch elevision.

Who lost a herd of elephants?
Big bo peep.

What did the baby elephant get when the daddy elephant sneezed?

Out of the way.

Why do elephants have short tails?

Because they can't remember long stories.

Why do elephants have trunks?

Because they'd look pretty stupid with suitcases.

Witty Waiter

Waiter, this soup tastes funny.

Why aren't you laughing, then?

Witty Waiter

Waiter, your thumb is in my soup!
Don't worry, it's not hot.

Waiter, there is a caterpillar on my dessert.
Don't worry sir, there's no extra charge.

Waiter, there is a fly in my soup!
Don't worry sir, that spider on your bread roll will soon get him.

Waiter, this coffee is disgusting, it tastes like earth.
Yes sir, it was ground yesterday.

Waiter, is there soup on the menu?

Not any more madam, I wiped it off.

Waiter, this boiled egg is bad.

Don't blame me sir, I only laid the table.

Waiter, there is a flea in my soup!

Well, tell him to hop it.

Waiter, there is a fly in my soup!

Yes sir, he committed insecticide this morning.

Waiter, there is a snail in my salad!

I'm sorry madam, I didn't realise you were vegetarian.

Waiter, there is a maggot swimming in my soup!

Don't worry sir, he won't last long in there.

Waiter, there is a slug in my roast dinner!

Didn't you see the sign madam – no pets allowed.

Waiter, why is there a bug in my wine?

You asked for a red with a little body in it.

Waiter, there are two flies in my soup!

That's OK, the extra one is on the house.

Waiter, what's this spider doing in my soup?

Why sir, it looks like it's learning to swim.

Waiter, there is a small slug in this lettuce.

I'm sorry madam, would you like me to fetch you a bigger one?

Waiter, my lunch is talking to me!

Yes, you ordered today's special – tongue sandwich.

Waiter, there is a slug in my sandwich!

Shhh, or everyone will want one.

Waiter, there is a spider in my bowl; I demand to speak to the manager.

That's no good, madam, he's scared of them too.

Waiter, why on earth is there a dead fly in my burger?

I don't know sir, perhaps it died after tasting it.

Waiter, what's this spider doing in my alphabet soup!

Probably learning to read sir.

Waiter, do you serve fatty birds?

Come and take a seat, madam, we serve everyone here.

Waiter, there is a dead fly in my chilli!

Yes sir, it's the heat that kills them.

Waiter, why is there a fly in my ice cream?

Perhaps he likes winter sports.

Waiter, there is a fly in the butter!

Yes sir, it's a butterfly.

Four Legs Good, Two Legs Baaaa

What do cows do for fun?
They go to the mooooovies.

What do you give a sick pig?
Oinkment.

Where can you find a horse with no legs?
Where you left it.

Why did the pig go to Vegas?
To play the slop machines.

Two cows are grazing in a field. One asks the other, 'Are you worried about this Mad Cow Disease?' The other replies, 'Why would I be? I'm a sheep.'

How long do chickens work?

Around the cluck.

Why don't chickens like people?

They beat eggs.

What do chickens grow on?

Eggplants.

Why are chickens always chatting?

Because talk is cheep.

What did the well-mannered sheep say at the field gate?

'After ewe.'

What did the chicken do when she saw a bucket of fried chicken?

She kicked the bucket.

Why did the calf miss school?

Because his parents were mooving.

How do cows cut the grass?

With a lawn-mooer.

How do you fit more pigs on your farm?

Build a sty-scraper.

What game do cows play at parties?

Moosical chairs.

What do you call a cow who lives in an igloo?

An Eskimoo.

What do drunk hens lay?

Scotch eggs.

How do you stop a rooster crowing on Sunday?

Eat him on Saturday.

What do you give a pony with a cold?

Cough stirrup.

Why did the bull rush?

Because it saw the cow slip.

Why did the ram fall over the cliff?

Because he didn't see the ewe turn.

What is a horse's favourite sport?

Stable tennis.

What is the easiest way to count a herd of cattle?

Use a cowculator.

What did the baby chick say when he saw his mother sitting on an orange?

Dad, look what mama laid.

What do you call a pig running around naked?

Streaky bacon.

What is the slowest horse in the world?

A clotheshorse.

Why do pigs never recover from illness?

Because you have to kill them before you cure them.

What do you call a pig who's been arrested for dangerous driving?

A road hog.

What do you call sheep that live in the same barn?

Pen friends.

How do chickens dance?

Chick to chick.

Which dance will a chicken not do?

The foxtrot.

What do you call a bull who tells jokes?

Laugh-a-bull.

What do chicken families do on Saturday afternoons?

They go on peck-nics.

Why did the chick disappoint his mother?

He wasn't what he was cracked up to be.

Is chicken soup good for your soul?

Not if you're the chicken.

Which day of the week do chickens hate most?

Fry-day.

What kind of tie does a pig wear?

A pig's tie.

What is the opposite of cock-a-doodle-doo?

Cock-a-doodle-don't.

Why was the lamb told off?

He didn't say 'thank ewe'.

How do pigs travel to hospital?

In a hambulance.

Birthday Belters

**What did the big birthday candle
say to the little candle?**

You're too young to go out.

What did the man buy for his wife's birthday when she said she wanted something with diamonds?

A pack of playing cards.

What did the jelly say to the miserable birthday cake?

What's eating you?

What's a rabbit's favourite party game?

Musical hares.

What's the best thing to buy an angry rhino for its birthday?

I'm not sure, but for your sake I hope it likes it.

Why do people put candles on the top of cakes?

Because you can't really put them on the bottom.

What kind of birthday cake is hard as a rock?

Marble cake.

What do snails do on their birthdays?

They shellebrate.

What did the old man wish for on his birthday?

No more birthdays.

Why didn't cavemen send birthday cards?

They could never get the stamps to stick to
the rocks.

**Where's the best place to look for a present
for your cat?**

In a catalogue.

**How do you make sure you always remember
your wife's birthday?**

Forget it once.

Rugby Romps

Why was Cinderella so bad at rugby?

She kept running away from the ball.

'Sorry I missed that conversion, captain,' said the player. 'I'm not sure what happened – it was such a simple shot. I could kick myself!' 'I wouldn't count on it,' replied the captain.

Two of the roughest rugby players were complaining about their coach's new tactics: 'It was much better in the past,' said one. 'All you had to remember was to kick ahead.' 'Yes,' said the other player, nodding in agreement. 'Any head would do!'

Why did the Irish rugby player kick his opponent twice?

To be sure, to be sure.

Why do rugby players date smart and beautiful women?

Because opposites attract.

Why couldn't the bicycle play in the rugby match?

Because it was two tyred.

What's the difference between the English rugby team and a box of Milk Tray?

You get better centres in the box of chocolates.

The fly half went up to his manager and said: 'I've got a great idea of how we could improve our game.' To which the manager replied: 'Brilliant! So when are you leaving?'

A rugby player approached the referee at the end of the match: 'My coach would like to know if there's a penalty for thinking.' 'No,' replied the ref. 'Well my captain thinks you're a prat, then,' said the player.

A man was seated in the front row at a rugby World Cup match with an empty seat beside him. Another man saw the empty seat and asked him: 'Could I have this seat?' 'Of course you can,' replied the man. 'It was meant for my wife, but she died very recently.' 'Why didn't you invite anyone to come with you?' asked the man. 'They're all attending the funeral,' he replied.

What do rugby players do when they start to lose their eyesight?

They become referees.

Fred had always played rugby in the Sunday league. This troubled his wife, so she asked the vicar whether it was a sin to play on Sunday. 'It's not a sin,' replied the vicar. 'The way he plays, it's a crime!'

The team's manager, coach, fullback and winger are flying to the cup final when the plane's engines die. The coach says, 'There are only three parachutes! The squad needs me – I'm taking one,' and jumps. The winger says, 'I'm the cleverest man on the team – I'm taking one,' and jumps. The manager says to the fullback, 'The last parachute is yours.' 'We can both have one,' he replies. 'The cleverest man on the team jumped with my kit bag on his back.'

The winger was clouted in the head during a tackle and knocked out cold. As the paramedic waved a towel at him and sprayed water on his face to revive him, he came round. 'Bloomin' 'eck,' he exclaimed. 'It was sunny when I fell over; this wind and rain's come from nowhere.'

What Do You Call...

What do you call a piece of cheese that isn't yours?

Nacho cheese.

What do you call a bee born in May?

A maybe.

What do you call a lion that has eaten your mother's sister?

An aunt-eater.

What do you call a flock of birds that fly in formation?

The red sparrows.

What do you call a one-legged lady?

Eileen.

What do you call a bee that never stops complaining?

A grumble bee.

What do you call a limbless man lying on your front doorstep?

Matt.

What do you call a limbless man hanging out in your pool?

Bob.

What do you call a joke book for chickens?

A yolk book.

What do you call a fish with no eyes?

A fsh.

What do you call a deer with no eyes?

No idea.

What do you call an elephant that has had too much to drink?

Trunk.

What do you call a big fish that makes you an offer you can't refuse?

The Codfather.

What do you call a parrot taking a shower?

Polly saturated.

What do you call an overweight ghost that haunts an opera house?

The fat tum of the opera.

What do you call a donkey with three legs?

A wonkey.

What do you call someone who makes tiny models of fish?

A scale modeller.

What do you call a dentist in the army?

A drill sergeant.

What do you call someone who dances on old cars?

A Morris dancer.

What do you call a show full of lions?

The mane event.

What do you call a rabbit sitting in a trifle?

A cream bun.

What do you call a sheep with no legs?
A cloud.

What do you call a dog that is always getting into fights?
A boxer.

What do you call the country's best dad?
Top of the pops.

What do you call a film about ducklings?
A duckumentary.

What do you call a very rude bird?
A mockingbird.

What do you call a chocolatey snack that poke fun at tunnelling mammals?

A mole-teaser.

What do you call a policeman with blonde hair?

A fair cop.

What do you call a Scottish parrot?

A macaw.

What do you call a fish riding a motorcycle?

A motor pike.

What do you call a traffic warden who never hands out fines?

A terrific warden.

What do you call an amazing artwork created by a rodent?

A mouseterpiece.

What do you call parrot food?

Polly filla.

What do you call a cat with eight legs that likes to swim?

An octopuss.

What do you call a clever duck?

A wise quacker.

What do you call a crazy chicken?

A cuckoo cluck.

What do you call it when you pass out after a late-night trip to the curry house?

A korma.

What do you call a man with a spade on his head?

Doug.

What do you call a man who's lost the spade from his head?

Douglas.

What do you call a lion wearing a cravat and a flower in its mane?

A dandy lion.

What do you call a cement-eating chicken?

A bricklayer.

What do you call a rabbit with fleas?

Bugs Bunny.

What do you call a man with a sat nav on his head?

Miles.

What do you call a man with a flat tyre on his head?

Jack.

What do you call a man with a number plate on his head?

Reg.

What do you call an ant with five pairs of eyes?

Antteneye.

What do you call a man with a toilet on his head?

Lou.

What do you call a woman with two toilets on her head?

Lulu.

What do you call a man with a prayer mat on his head?

Neil.

What do you call an elephant that flies?

A jumbo jet.

What do you call a woman with a radiator on her head?

Anita.

What do you call a woman with thatch on her head?

Ruth.

What do you call a man with a plastic bag on his head?

Russell.

What do you call a snake that gets you into trouble?

A grass snake.

What do you call a man who's been scratched by your cat?

Claude.

What do you call a man with a seagull on his head?

Cliff.

What do you call a girl with a frog on her head?

Lily.

What do you call a girl who keeps getting hit by footballs?

Annette.

What do you call a masked horseman with a pleasant aroma?

The Cologne Ranger.

What do you call a snake that works for the government?

A civil serpent.

What do you call a woman with a snail on her back?

Shelley.

What do you call a man with a rucksack covered in salt and pepper?

A seasoned traveller.

What do you call a cat that's swallowed a duck?

A duck-filled fatty puss.

What do you give to a deer with indigestion?

Elk-a-seltzer.

What do you call a dog in jeans and a sweater?

A plain-clothes police dog.

What do you call a row of rabbits running away from you?

A receding hare-line.

What do you call a 100-year-old ant?

An antique.

What do you call two banana skins?

A pair of slippers.

What do you call a blind dinosaur?

Do-you-think-he-saurus.

What do you call a girl with burgers cooking on her head?

Barbie.

What do you call a litter of dogs that have just come in from the snow?

Slush puppies.

**What do you call a woman with a strong
wind on her head?**

Gail.

**What do you call a man covered in meat,
sliced carrots and a thick gravy?**

Stu.

What do you call a guard with 100 legs?

A sentrypede.

**What do you call a sweater that's jumping up
and down?**

A bungee jumper.

What do you call a sleeping male cow?

A bull-dozer.

Buzz Buzz. Who's There?

What goes zzub, zzub?

A bee flying backwards.

What kind of bees make milk?
Boobies.

Where did Noah keep his bees?
In the ark hives.

Why was the fly dancing on the top of the lemonade bottle?
Because the label said 'Twist to open'.

What flies around your light at night and can bite off your head?
A tiger moth.

What games do ants play with elephants?
Squash.

Why are ant colonies free from disease?

Because they are full of antibodies.

What kind of ant is good at maths?

An accountant.

How many ants are needed to fill an apartment?

Ten ants.

What do bees do if they want to use public transport?

Wait at a buzz stop.

What does a queen bee do when she burps?

She issues a royal pardon.

Why did the bee start talking poetry?

He was waxing lyrical.

What's a bee's favourite TV show?

Never Mind the Buzzcocks.

Who is the popular children's author for bees?

Bee-trix Potter.

What did a mother bee say to her naughty son?

Bee-hive yourself.

Why do bees hum?

Because they've forgotten the words.

What kind of bee drops things?

A fumble bee.

What did the bee say to the flower?

Hello honey.

What did the confused bee say?

To bee or not to bee.

What bee is good for your health?

Vitamin bee.

What kind of bee should speak up?

A mumble bee.

What does a bee get at a burger bar?

A humburger.

What did the spider say to the bee?

Your honey or your life.

Who is a bee's favourite pop group?

The Bee Gees.

Why do bees have sticky hair?

Because of the honey combs.

Where do bees go on holiday?

Stingapore.

Why did the queen bee kick out all the other bees?

Because they kept droning on.

What does a bee say before it stings you?

This is going to hurt me a lot more than it hurts you.

Which pillar doesn't need holding up?

A caterpillar.

What does a caterpillar do on New Year's Day?

Turns over a new leaf.

What goes 99… clonk, 99… clonk, 99… clonk?

A centipede with a wooden leg.

Why was the centipede dropped from the insect football team?

He took too long to put his boots on.

What is worse than a shark with toothache?

A centipede with athlete's foot.

What has fifty legs but cant walk?

Half a centipede.

What did the boy centipede say to the girl centipede?

You've got a lovely pair of legs, you've got a lovely pair of legs, you've got a lovely pair of legs…

What kind of wig can hear?

An earwig.

What did the earwig say as it fell down the stairs?

Ear we go.

What did the clean dog say to the flea?

Long time no flea.

What is a flea's favourite book?

The Itch-hikers Guide to the Galaxy.

Why were the flies playing football in a saucer?

They were playing for the cup.

What did the firefly say as he was leaving?

Got to glow now.

What is green and can jump a mile in a minute?

A grasshopper with hiccups.

What has antlers and sucks blood?

A moose-quito.

What do insects learn at school?

Mothmatics.

What is a myth?

A female moth.

Why did the moth nibble a hole in the carpet?

He wanted to see the floor show.

What's the biggest moth that's ever lived?

A mammoth.

What happened when the spider got angry?

He went up the wall.

**How do you know your kitchen floor
is dirty?**

The slugs leave a trail on the floor that reads
'clean me'.

What was the snail doing on the motorway?

About one mile a day.

How do snails get their shells so shiny?

They use snail varnish.

What do you do when two snails have a fight?

Leave them to slug it out.

What did the maggot say to his friend when he got stuck in an apple?

Worm your way out of that one.

How can you tell which end of a worm is which?

Tickle it in the middle and see which end laughs.

Why was the glow-worm unhappy?

Because her children weren't that bright.

What did one maggot say to another?

What's a nice maggot like you doing in a joint like this?

What did the woodworm say to the chair?

It's been nice gnawing you.

Why are glow-worms good to carry in your bag?

They can lighten your load.

Two ants were sprinting across the top of a cereal box. One screamed to the other, 'Why are we running so fast?' The other one shouted back, 'Because it says "tear along the dotted line"!'

Everybody Talks About the Weather

Did you hear about the cows that got caught up in a tornado?

It was an udder disaster.

What did one tornado say to the other?

'Let's twist again, like we did last summer.'

Why did the woman run outside with her purse open?

Because she heard there would be some change in the weather.

Which animal should you never invite to your barbeque?

A reindeer.

What is fowl weather?

When it starts raining chickens and ducks.

How did the woman lose her husband when they were eating ice lollies?

He got caught up in a Twister.

What's the difference between a horse and the weather?

One is reined up and the other rains down.

What did one raindrop say to the other raindrop?

My plop is bigger than your plop.

What's worse than raining cats and dogs?

Hailing taxis.

What do you have to be careful of when it rains cats and dogs?

Not to step in a poodle.

What did one hurricane say to the other hurricane?

'I've got my eye on you.'

What did one lightning bolt say to the other lightning bolt?

You're shocking.

'You never get anything right,' complained the
teacher. 'What job do you think you'll be able to do
when you leave school?' 'Well,' replied the pupil, 'I
want to be a weather forecaster.'

How do sheep stay warm in winter?
Central bleating.

Under Da Sea

Why did the lobster blush?

Because the sea weed.

What's long, slippery and likes to dance?

A conga eel.

What's round, chocolatey and found in the ocean?

An oyster egg.

Where are whales weighed?

At a whale weigh station.

Why wouldn't you want to fight an octopus?

They're very well armed.

How do you stop a fish from smelling?

Cut its nose off.

Where do shellfish go to borrow money?

To the prawn broker.

Which fish can perform operations?

A sturgeon.

What happened to the shark that swallowed a bunch of keys?

He got lockjaw.

Where do little fish go every morning?

To plaice school.

What is the saddest creature in the sea?

The blue whale.

Where do you find a down-and-out octopus?

On squid row.

What do you give a fish that is hard of hearing?

A herring aid.

Which fish comes out at night?

A starfish.

Which fish go to heaven when they die?

Angelfish.

What kind of fish goes well with ice cream?

Jellyfish.

What is a dolphin's favourite TV show?
Whale of fortune.

How do fish borrow money?
They go to a loan shark.

Who held the baby octopus to ransom?
Squidnappers.

What was the Tsar of Russia's favourite fish?
Tsardines.

How do fish get to school?
By octobus.

What fish do road workers use?

Pneumatic krill.

**Why shouldn't little fish go out alone
at night?**

In case they bump into Jack the Kipper.

What did the boy fish say to his girlfriend?

Your plaice or mine?

Where does seaweed look for work?

In the 'kelp wanted' ads.

One kipper says to another, 'Smoking is bad for you.' The other replies, 'Don't worry, I've been cured.'

What kind of fish is useful in freezing weather?
Skate.

What is the best way to communicate with a fish?
Drop it a line.

An Englishman, an Irishman and a Scotsman

An Englishman, an Irishman and a Scotsman ordered a pint of Guinness each at the pub. Just as they were about to drink, a fly landed in each of their glasses. The Englishman, disgusted, refused to drink his pint. The Scotsman fished his fly out and started sipping, while the Irishman yanked the fly out of his drink and yelled, 'Spit out my beer you thieving little insect!'

An Englishman, a Welshman and an Irishman come across a wise man in the desert. He tells them that whatever they shout out when they jump over the next sand dune, they will land in it on the other side. The Englishman runs to the sand dune and jumps, shouting 'Gold!' and sure enough lands in a pile of gold coins. The Welshman follows in quick pursuit screaming 'Diamonds!' at the top of his lungs, and finds himself surrounded by them. Then the Irishman launches himself from the top of the dune and screams, 'Weeeeeeeee!'

An Englishman, an Irishman and a Scotsman are discussing their relationships. 'I think my girlfriend's cheating on me with a copper, because I found some handcuffs under her bed last night,' says the Englishman. 'I think mine's cheating on me with a jockey, because I found a whip under her bed last night,' admits the Scotsman. 'I don't think my girlfriend's cheating on me,' says the Irishman, 'but she's probably sick, because I found a doctor under her bed last night.'

An Englishman, a Frenchman and an Irishman are talking about their children in the pub. 'My son was born on St George's Day,' explains the Englishman, 'so we called him George.' 'What a coincidence,' says the Frenchman, 'my daughter was born on St Valentine's Day, so we called her Valentine!' 'That's incredible,' says the Irishman in disbelief. 'We did the exact same thing for our son, Pancake!'

Three Englishmen stroll into a pub and decide to pick a fight with a lone Welshman at the bar. 'I know how to rile him up,' says the first Englishman, and he goes over to him and says, 'St David was a girl.' The Welshman replies, 'Ah, yes.' The second Englishman goes over and tries again, saying, 'St David was an idiot.' 'Ah, yes,' the Welshman replies once more. The third Englishman, determined to annoy the Welshman, marches over and shouts, 'St David was an Englishman!' The Welshman sets down his drink, turns, and says, 'Yes, that's what your mates were trying to tell me.'

A Scotsman, an Irishman and an Englishman are sentenced to one year of solitary confinement in prison, but are allowed to take a year's supply of anything with them. The Scotsman takes in battered Mars bars, the Irishman chooses Guinness and the Englishman requests cigarettes. A year later, the Scotsman emerges from his cell and has a heart attack minutes later. The Irishman staggers out and dies from liver failure. Then the Englishman is released. He walks quickly out of his cell, turns to the guards and says, 'I don't suppose anyone has a light, do they?'

An Englishman, an Irishman and a Scotsman are about to face the firing squad. 'Before we kill you,' says their foreign captor, 'we will grant you one final wish.' After some consideration, the Englishman says, 'I'd like to hear "God Save the Queen" to remind me of home, and throw in some Morris dancers, too.' The Irishman then responds, 'And I would like a full-length performance of *Riverdance*.' Reaching his decision almost immediately, the Scotsman announces, 'I'd like to be shot first.'

An Englishman, an Irishman and a Scotsman are working on a building site. The Englishman opens his lunchbox and says, 'If I get one more ham sandwich, I'm going to jump off this building.' The Scotsman opens his and says, 'Well, if I get one more chicken sandwich I'm going to kill myself, too.' The Irishman says, 'You're right, if I get cheese again, I'm jumping with you.' The next day the three men get the same lunches and act out their suicide pact. At their funeral the Englishman's and Scotsman's wives declare, 'If only we'd known how much they hated those sandwiches we'd made.' The Irishman's wife, confused, says, 'Well, I don't know why my husband jumped – he made his own sandwiches.'

An Englishman, an Irishman and a Scotsman come across a genie who grants them one wish each. The Scotsman says, 'I am a fisherman and so I wish for the seas to be filled with fish,' and his wish is instantly granted. The Englishman says, 'I love my country and wish for a wall to be built around England, protecting it from future invasion.' Immediately, his wish is also granted. The Irishman says to the genie, 'Tell me about this wall.' 'It's about 200 feet high and 50 feet thick, so nothing can get in or out,' responds the genie. The Irishman smiles and replies, 'Please fill it up with water.'

An Englishman, an Irishman and a Scotsman were stranded on a mountain. A fairy godmother appeared and said she would turn each of them into a bird of their choice to get off the mountain safely. The Englishman said, 'I would like to be a swan,' and at once he was transformed and flew gracefully to England. The Scotsman said, 'I would like to be a Golden Eagle,' and he too was transformed and went gliding safely home. 'And what bird do you choose?' the fairy godmother asked the Irishman. He thought about it for a minute and said, 'A penguin.'

An Englishman, an Irishman and a Scotsman are on the run from the police. They find an old warehouse, run inside and crawl into three large potato sacks. The police catch up and start searching the warehouse. One policeman kicks the nearest sack and the Englishman calls out, 'Woof, woof!' The copper says, 'It's only a dog,' and kicks the second sack. 'Meow, meow!' cries out the Scotsman. 'Just a cat,' the copper says. He walks over to the third sack and kicks it hard. The Irishman yells out, 'Potatoes, potatoes!'

An Englishman, an Irishman and a Scotsman are chatting about their tea-drinking habits. 'I always stir my tea with my left hand,' says the Englishman. 'That's funny, I always stir my tea with my right hand,' says the Scotsman. 'How about you?' he asks the Irishman. 'Oh me?' says the Irishman. 'I always use a spoon.'

An Englishman, an Irishman and a Scotsman can't get tickets for the Olympics. But when the Englishman spots a building site near the entrance, he has a great idea. Grabbing a scaffolding pole he walks to the gate, announces, 'Samuels, pole vault!' and the guards let him walk through. The Scotsman tries his luck and walks through with a sledgehammer, declaring, 'Macdonald, hammer!' Then the Irishman takes his turn and, grabbing a roll of barbed wire, walks to the gate and says, 'O'Riley, fencing!'

Stomach Fillers

What did the nut say when he sneezed?

Cashew!

**What's orange, long and sounds like
a parrot?**

A carrot.

Why was the soup so expensive?

Because there were twenty-four carrots in it.

Why did the bun whistle?

Because he saw the hot dog.

**What did the big tomato say to his little
brother?**

Ketchup.

**What did the salt say to the melodramatic
fry-up?**

Stop eggs-aggerating.

What did the photographer say to the curdled milk?

'Say, "Cheese!"'

What's white, round and can't stop giggling?

A tickled onion.

What's the worst vegetable to find on a boat?

A leek.

What's white, sugary and swings through the trees?

A meringue-utan.

What jumps from cake to cake and tastes like almonds?

Tarzipan.

Why wasn't the bacon allowed to compete in the swimming competition?

It was a sausage meet.

What kind of biscuit can take you to an exotic location?

A plain biscuit.

Why did the raspberries cry?

Because they were in a jam.

Why did the police come round for breakfast?

Because someone had poached the eggs.

When the stranded plane-crash survivors turned to cannibalism, why didn't they eat they comedian?

Because he tasted funny.

What did the gunman say before he shot the loaf of bread?

You're toast!

Two peanuts walk into a bar.

One was a salted.

Why wasn't the orange annoyed when he couldn't open the biscuit tin?

Because the lemon curd.

Two muffins were in the oven. Suddenly, one of them shouted, 'Man! It's hot in here!' The other muffin pointed and said, 'Look! A talking muffin!'

What did the spectator say when the cake sprinted past?

Scone.

Why did the ice scream?

Because he heard the lolly pop.

A dairy factory worker lost her job when she fell in a vat.

She was sacked for getting in the whey.

What flies and wobbles?

A jellycopter.

Why do the French love eating snails?

Because they can't stand fast food.

Why don't gingerbread men wear shorts?

Because their legs are crumby.

Why are prunes worth buying?

You get a good run for your money.

How did the man drown in the fruit cake?

He was pulled under by a strong currant.

Why did the iced bun blush?

Because he'd just popped his cherry.

Did you hear about what happened in the biscuit tin? The bandit knocked the penguin out with a club, tied him to a wagon wheel with a blue ribbon and made a quick breakaway in a taxi!

Why couldn't the sesame seed leave the blackjack table?

He was on a roll.

What should you feed a hungry computer?

Chips. One byte at a time.

Why did the bread rush down the hill?

Because he saw the cheese roll.

What inspired the salad to take up cooking?
Watching the pasta bake.

**What happened to the jug of milk in
the punch-up?**
He got creamed.

**What do cannibals order when they have
a takeaway?**
Pizza with everyone on it.

What do astronauts put in their sandwiches?
Launch meat.

Why couldn't the burger stop smiling?

He was in a Happy Meal.

Why did the fries turn the music up?

To see the milk shake.

Why is a sofa like a roast chicken?

Because they're both full of stuffing.

Your Monkey or Your Life

Why was the monkey lonely?

Because the banana split.

Why do gorillas have big nostrils?

Where else are they going to put those big fingers?

Why did the orang-utan get told off at school?

He was monkeying around.

What did the monkey say when he accidentally cut his tail in half?

It won't be long now.

Why did the chimp go to the primate mental home?

Because his mum asked him to pick up some monkey nuts.

Why was the monkey scared to go to the barbeque?

Because she thought they might gorilla.

What do you call a monkey at the top of the tree?

A branch manager.

Where do monkeys hear rumours?

On the apevine.

A pet monkey needed a brain transplant, and the vet told the owners it would cost £500,000 for a male brain and £200,000 for a female brain. 'Why the price difference?' asked the owners. 'It's standard pricing practice,' the vet replied. 'We have to mark down the female brains because they've been used.'

Mad Men

What's the difference between a man and E.T. ?

E.T. phoned home.

What is the difference between men and government bonds?

Bonds mature.

Why are blonde jokes so short?

So men can remember them.

Why do men want to meet women?

Because otherwise their shirts would be creased.

Why are dogs better than boyfriends?

After a year, they're still pleased to see you.

What's a man's idea of housework?

Lifting his legs so you can vacuum.

Why did God create Eve?

Because he realised all the mistakes he'd made first
time round.

How do men exercise at the beach?

By sucking in their bellies every time they see
a bikini.

What do men and beer bottles have
in common?

They are both empty from the neck up.

One woman says to another, 'I was dating a man who said he was God's gift to women.' Her friend asks, 'What happened?' The woman replies, 'I exchanged him.'

What should you get for the man who has everything?

A woman to show him how to make it work.

How long is a piece of string?

That depends, how lazy is the man whose job it is to cut it?

Why do black widow spiders kill their males after mating?

To avoid the snoring.

How do men plan for the future?

They buy two cases of beer and put one in the cooler by the sofa.

Why is going to the circus better than going out to a singles bar?

At the circus, the clowns don't talk.

Anyone for Tennis?

Why couldn't the man light the fire?

He was trying to use a tennis match.

What do you serve but not eat?

A tennis ball.

Why should you never fall in love with a tennis player?

'Love' means nothing to them.

Why aren't fish good at tennis?

They don't like getting close to the net.

What is the definition of endless love?

Ray Charles and Stevie Wonder playing tennis.

A tennis player popped his lucky tennis
ball into his shorts' pocket after a
successful match and headed back to the
clubhouse. On his way to the changing
rooms he passed a blonde, who eyed
the bulge in his shorts before asking,
'What's that?' 'Tennis ball,' replied
the tennis player. 'Oh,' said the blonde
sympathetically, 'that must be painful... I
had tennis elbow once.'

Why is tennis such a noisy sport?
Because the players all raise a racket.

Where do ghosts play tennis?
On a tennis corpse!

Why did the tennis player hit his first serve into the net?
He didn't want to be cheated out of his second shot.

Which US state is famous for tennis?
Tennis-see.

A middle-aged man was told by his doctor he needed to exercise more, and so decided to take up tennis. After a few weeks a mate asked how it was going. 'It's OK,' replied the man. 'When I'm on the court and I see the ball speeding my way, my brain immediately says, "To the corner! Back hand! To the net! Smash!" But then my body says, "Who? Me? You must be kidding!"'

What do you call an intelligent tennis player?

A racket scientist.

What do you get if you cross a skunk and a pair of tennis rackets?

Ping pong!

What time does Sean Connery get up to play his favourite sport?

Tennish.

What's the Difference Between...

What's the difference between a fish and a piano?

You can't tuna fish.

What's the difference between a mosquito and a fly?

Try zipping up a mosquito.

What's the difference between a lawyer and a leech?

When you die, a leech will stop sucking your blood and drop off.

What's the difference between an inflatable dartboard and a kilo of lard?

One is a fat lot of good and the other is a good lot of fat.

What's the difference between an injured lion and an English summer's day?

One roars with pain and the other pours with rain.

What's the difference between a well-dressed man and a tired dog?

One wears a suit and tie, the other just pants.

What's the difference between a flea and a wolf?

One prowls on the hairy and the other howls on the prairie.

What's the difference between a fly and a bird?

A bird can fly but a fly can't bird.

What's the difference between ignorance and apathy?

I don't know, and I don't care.

What's the difference between a lawyer and an angry rhinoceros?

The lawyer charges more.

What's the difference between an angry circus owner and a Roman barber?

One is a raving showman, and the other is a shaving Roman.

What's the difference between a man and a chimpanzee?

One is hairy, smelly and is always scratching its bum and the other is a chimpanzee.

What's the difference between a duck and a cow?

They both swim, except for the cow.

What's the difference between roast beef and pea soup?

Anyone can roast beef.

What's the difference between a viola and a trampoline?

You take your shoes off to jump on a trampoline.

Christmas Crackers

Why did the snowman call his dog Frost?

Because Frost bites.

Two snowmen are standing in a field. One says to the other, 'Do you smell carrots?'

What do tigers sing at Christmas?

'Jungle bells, jungle bells...'

Why did the turkey cross the road?

Because he heard Christmas was cancelled over there.

How do snowmen get to work?

By icicle.

What do you get if you cross a tiger with Father Christmas?

Santa Claws.

What do angry rodents send each other for Christmas?

Cross mouse cards.

What do you call a woman with Christmas decorations on her head?

Carol.

Why did the pupil do so badly in January?

Everything gets marked down after Christmas.

Two blonde girls were spotted shivering in their car at an abandoned drive-in cinema on Christmas Day. They went to see 'Closed for the winter'.

What did the pirate say when he dressed up as Santa?

Ho, ho, ho and a bottle of rum.

What do you get if you cross a vampire with a snowman?

Frostbite.

What did Father Christmas's wife say during a thunderstorm?

'Come and look at the rain, dear.'

**What's the difference between a snowman
and a snowwoman?**

Snowballs.

Why is Christmas like a day at work?

You do all the work and a fat man in a suit gets all
the credit.

**What do Christmas trees do when winter
is over?**

They pine a lot.

Have you enjoyed this book? If so, why not write a review
on your favourite website?

Thanks very much for buying this Summersdale book.

www.summersdale.com